VOLUME

5

THE
AMERICAN HERITAGE
BOOK OF THE
PRESIDENTS
AND FAMOUS AMERICANS

★ ★ ★ ★ ★

FRANKLIN PIERCE

JAMES BUCHANAN

ABRAHAM LINCOLN

CREATED AND DESIGNED BY THE EDITORS OF
AMERICAN HERITAGE
The Magazine of History

12-VOLUME EDITION PUBLISHED BY
DELL PUBLISHING CO., INC., NEW YORK, N.Y.

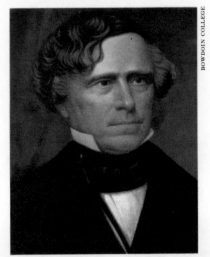

Franklin Pierce

James Buchanan

Abraham Lincoln

CONTENTS
OF VOLUME FIVE

FAMOUS AMERICANS

FRANKLIN PIERCE

The wife of Senator Clement Claiborne Clay of Alabama recalled that before Franklin Pierce became President of the United States she had "seen him bound up the stairs with the elasticity of a schoolboy. He went out after four years," she added, "a staid and grave man, on whom the stamp of care and illness was ineradicably impressed." So, she might have said, was the stamp of failure.

If the storm that climaxed in the Civil War can be likened to a hurricane, then Franklin Pierce came to the White House in the hurricane's eye. To many, the Compromise of 1850 seemed to have settled the major differences between North and South. Indeed, when Charles Sumner of Massachusetts arrived in the Senate in 1851, Thomas Hart Benton of Missouri told him, "You have come upon the scene too late, sir. There is nothing left to settle except petty, sectional disturbances over slavery."

But the quiet was deceptive. The eye of the hurricane was moving past, and Pierce—charming, kind, introspective, an old-fashioned Democratic party regular raised in the political backwater of New Hampshire—would be battered by the storm and swept away. He never comprehended the central moral issue of the day: slavery. He could not understand the abolitionists and for years fought them for stirring up trouble. Like many other men dedicated to the preservation of the Union, he could not see that the Compromise of 1850—particularly that part of it known as the Fugitive Slave Law—contained the seeds of continued bitterness between the sections; it created moral indignation in the North and fed the abolition movement, which in turn aroused the South. How little of this Pierce understood was indicated by his inaugural pledge to the country to preserve the Union by adhering to the Compromise. In many ways, Pierce was an anachronistic figure. His ideals,

Franklin Pierce, by G. P. A. Healy

Bennie Pierce, seen above with his mother when he was nine, was killed before his twelfth birthday.

learned from his father (who had been a general during the Revolutionary War), were those of a far less complicated age. His heroes were the men who had signed the Constitution of the United States, and he longed for a return to the conciliatory spirit that had marked the Constitutional Convention of 1787, seventeen years before his own birth on November 23, 1804, in Hillsboro, New Hampshire.

Politically speaking, Pierce came into the world with a silver spoon in his mouth: his father was a leading figure in the state and was subsequently its governor. A lawyer at twenty-two, the future President became a state legislator two years later. He was speaker of the legislature at twenty-six, a member of Congress at twenty-nine, and a senator at thirty-three. But though his mastery of New Hampshire politics led to the 1852 presidential nomination, it did not train him to run a national party that was splitting along sectional lines. Nor was he emotionally equipped. Pierce was a follower, not a leader. He followed the advice of his father and of the leaders of his party, right

up to his entry into the White House. Always, he was too anxious to please others.

His home life was unsatisfactory: his wife, the former Jane Means Appleton, daughter of the president of Bowdoin College, Pierce's alma mater, did not like either Washington or politics. She was a withdrawn, deeply religious neurotic and frequently an invalid. In deference to her, Pierce retired from the national scene in 1842 and returned to New Hampshire to practice law. But he continued to participate in state politics, with a brief hiatus during the Mexican War, when he served as a brigadier general in Winfield Scott's drive on Mexico City.

Pierce capped his New Hampshire achievements in 1850 and 1851 when his party's gubernatorial candidate began to show free-soil sympathies. Pierce led the move to replace him with a man who supported compromise. The latter's victory in the subsequent election was regarded throughout the nation, and especially in the South, as a triumph for Pierce. As the 1852 nominating convention approached, he began to loom as a dark-horse alternative to the Democratic front-runners—Lewis Cass, Stephen Douglas, James Buchanan, William O. Butler, and William Marcy—who seemed destined to deadlock the convention. Because he knew his wife would not approve, Pierce could not show much enthusiasm; he did not, however, repudiate the use of his name at the convention, and his supporters managed to win the nomination for him, as a compromise candidate, on the forty-ninth ballot. According to his friend Nathaniel Hawthorne, Pierce received the news "with no thrill of joy, but a sadness." When a rider brought them the report, Mrs. Pierce fainted. The strength and the openness of her antipathy to her husband's political ambitions were revealed in a letter that her eleven-year-old son, Bennie, wrote to her: "Edward brought the news . . . that Father is a candidate for the Presidency. I hope he won't be elected for I should not like to be at Washington and I know you would not either."

In the campaign that followed, Pierce

said and wrote little, as was the custom of the period, allowing the party chiefs to garner votes for him. They nicknamed him Young Hickory, casting back to the glorious days of the Democratic party. In the fall of 1852, he defeated the Whig candidate, General Winfield Scott, 254 electoral votes to 42. His popular-vote margin was only about 216,000, but the defeat effectively put an end to the Whig party.

"I have come seriously to the conclusion," wrote Hawthorne about the President-elect, "that he has in him many of the chief elements of a great ruler. His talents are administrative, he has a subtle faculty of making affairs roll onward according to his will, and of influencing their course without showing any trace of his action. . . . He is deep, deep, deep."

Pierce immediately began to lay plans for his administration: it would have a strong foreign policy; it would seek peaceful expansion; it would be frugal and honest; it would stand by strict construction, the Compromise, and the rights of the Southern states. His Cabinet, he hoped, would unify the unstable party organization. Eventually it included both the breakaway Barnburner elements and some Southern states' rights advocates; notable among the latter was Jefferson Davis, the Secretary of War.

The vigor with which he pursued his pre-inaugural plans came to an abrupt end in January, 1853. As the Pierces traveled from Boston to Concord, New Hampshire, the railroad car in which they were riding rolled off the track and their young son, Bennie, was killed. The parents were virtually unhurt, but at that instant their lives were shattered. Bennie was the third child they had lost. Their first son had died at the age of three days, and another had succumbed to typhus when he was four. Bennie had been their pride and the center of their marriage. The melancholy Mrs. Pierce interpreted the tragedy as a sign from God that her husband was not to be preoccupied with thoughts of a family so that he could better carry out the responsibilities of the Presidency. From then on, Jane Pierce rarely made public appearances, and when she did, it was with an air of martyred sadness.

Pierce was smothered by guilt and despair. Those who dealt with him found him timid and distracted. His journey to Washington for the inauguration was characteristic. Mrs. Pierce did not accompany him. Stopping off in New York, he avoided the crowds that had turned out to greet him. He did the same in Washington; instead of allowing himself to be welcomed by the mayor, he got off at the rear of the train and went to the Willard Hotel, where he stayed until the inauguration on March 4.

Yet his Inaugural Address showed flashes of positiveness. Always a skillful speaker, he had committed the speech to memory— the first President to do so. In it he outlined his goals and drew admiration from his audience for his choice of words as much as for his sentiments. In deference to Pierce's mourning, there was no inaugural ball, but a swarm of people descended on the White House for a reception that lasted all afternoon. That evening the new President and his private secretary, Sidney Webster, lit a candle and searched through the Mansion for a place to sleep; nothing was ready for them. At last Pierce gave up. He pointed to one room and said to Webster, "You had better turn in here and I will find a bed across the hall."

Mrs. Pierce arrived soon after, accompanied by her aunt, Mrs. Abby Kent Means —who became the official White House hostess in lieu of the First Lady—and took to her bedroom, where she wrote pathetic notes to her dead Bennie. The Executive Mansion took on an air of somber New England piety, with Mrs. Pierce asking the servants to attend church "for her sake" each Sunday. One visitor commented that "everything in that mansion seems cold and cheerless. I have seen hundreds of log cabins which seemed to contain more happiness."

Meanwhile, the President met the first problems of his administration. Patronage was one. Distributing the spoils of government to deserving party members was made particularly difficult by the existence of bickering factions within the party. Pierce could not please one group without angering another. His job was made no easier by his deep desire to please everyone. He backed and filled, listened to advice from all quarters, and agreed on appointments one day and changed his mind the next. His difficulties with appointments helped weaken his position with Democrats of all stripes.

There were troubling policy questions as well, almost all of which were complicated by sectional debate. Pierce bent all his efforts toward compromise, trying to avoid clashes. But unfortunately this meant compromising in favor of the South, which seriously threatened to break up the Union. To begin with, there was the question of a transcontinental railroad. The month Pierce was inaugurated, Congress authorized the War Department, under Jefferson Davis, to survey four transcontinental railroad routes. Southerners thought that the best route might be one running from New Orleans, across Texas and the New Mexico Territory, to San Diego. In May, Pierce's advisers prevailed upon him to negotiate with Mexico for a small portion of territory across which the railroad might run, and in December James Gadsden signed a treaty with Mexico in which the United States agreed to purchase a 29,640-square-mile rectangle of land for $15,000,000—a price later reduced by a third. However, the land speculations of many powerful men, not a few of whom were members of the national legislature, were also involved. This group included Senator Stephen Douglas, the "little giant" from Illinois, who began plumping for a central route out of Chicago that followed emigration trails west and went through the Great Plains, which were not yet territorialized. To clear the way for this line, his Senate committee issued a bill establishing the Territory of Nebraska. Since an earlier attempt to organize Nebraska had not won support from the South, and since there were indications that this new bill would fail for the same reason, Douglas tried to draw Southern votes to his side by including in the bill the proviso that the slave or free

status of the territory would be settled by its inhabitants. But the Great Plains had been closed to slavery by the Missouri Compromise, and the effect of Douglas' Nebraska Act would be to repeal *ipso facto* that Compromise. Southern senators soon called for an amendment to repeal the Missouri Compromise outright. Pierce did not favor the amendment, preferring to force the question into the Supreme Court where, he was positive, the Compromise would be declared unconstitutional. But the Southern bloc in the Senate would not back down, and Pierce found himself trapped; his administration's success depended on the support of Southern Democrats. With deep misgivings, Pierce went along with their amendment. The new bill also included division of the territory into Kansas and Nebraska. It was therefore possible that the southernmost, Kansas, would become a slave state through emigration from Missouri. Having made an unpleasant choice, Pierce threw his support completely behind the Kansas-Nebraska Act, and he whipped enough Democratic dissenters into line to win its passage. At the time, he felt he had achieved a major victory.

Kansas then became the scene of a bitter civil war, as settlers and land speculators from the slave state of Missouri and from abolitionist New England flocked into the territory and fought for control of the government. In the first two elections, "border ruffians" from Missouri flooded over the state line and elected proslavery representatives. This government set up its capital at Lecompton and was recognized as official by the territorial governor (who feared that he would be killed if he acted otherwise); it was therefore recognized by President Pierce. The antislavery men countered by creating another government in Topeka.

The Kansas-Nebraska Act was the great tragedy of Pierce's administration. It cost him, first, control of his party: Northern Democrats, their passions aroused by the repeal of the Missouri Compromise, defected; and Southern Democrats quickly grew impatient at the President's consequent inability to pass other pro-South measures. Then it cost the Democrats control of the House, as Know-Nothings and the new, antislavery Republican party made notable gains in the mid-term elections.

Increasingly hobbled by the sectional breakup inside and outside his party, Pierce struggled to cope with numerous other problems. The annexation of Cuba had long been urged by Southerners, and James K. Polk had tried with no success to buy it from Spain. The situation was complicated for Pierce by the belligerent attitude of certain segments of the American public; they were for taking whatever they wanted by force, and they organized filibustering expeditions that Pierce did not know how to handle. Furthermore, there were indications that Britain and France were encouraging Spain to free the slaves in Cuba, with an eye toward preventing American expansion southward; the island would thus appear less attractive to those Southerners who were planning to turn it into a slave state. Spain herself tended to excoriate relations with the United States, and on the 28th of February, 1854, Cuban authorities committed the blunder of seizing the cargo of an American ship for a minor violation of the rules of the port of Havana. This stirred anti-Spanish feelings in the United States and brought forth loud demands for war. Secretary of State William L. Marcy prevailed with cooler counsel, however. In a comic postlude, the American ministers to Spain, France, and Great Britain, under instructions to plan diplomatic maneuvers to wrench Cuba from Spain, met in Ostend and issued a manifesto, which was not a united diplomatic policy, but rather a suggestion that the United States either buy the island or, if Spain would not sell, wrest it from her. Pierce was right back where he had started, with Northerners angry at his attempts to annex a possible slave state.

The President also considered the annexation of Hawaii. A treaty was drafted in November, 1854, which would bring the island kingdom into the Union as a state in return for cash to the royal family, but Pierce knew the treaty would have difficulty in the Sen-

WILLIAM R. KING

In March, 1853, William R. King was sworn into the Vice Presidency under "the clear sky of the tropics." By a special act of Congress, the Vice President-elect, suffering from tuberculosis, was permitted to take the oath of office in Havana, where he was struggling to regain his health. In April he died, never having served in the office for which his long years in Congress had so ably prepared him. A graduate of the University of North Carolina, King was admitted to the bar in 1806 and was elected to the House of Representatives four years later. In 1818 he moved to Alabama. Representing his state in the Senate from 1820 to 1844, he chaired a committee on public lands, became an ardent follower of Jackson, and served as president pro tempore of the Senate for five years. In 1844 President Tyler appointed him minister to France, where he worked to prevent French interference in the annexation of Texas. Returning to the Senate in 1848, he supported the Compromise of 1850, worked toward the ratification of the Clayton-Bulwer Treaty, and, when Fillmore acceded to the Presidency, became president of the Senate. When the Democratic convention met in 1852, the delegates settled on the winning team of "gallant Pierce and King." King's death one month after his inauguration left the United States without a Vice President until Kentucky's John C. Breckinridge assumed the office in 1857.

ate if presented there for approval. Britain was against it; France seemed to be also. At the least, the treaty would have to be rewritten. But before it could be, the Hawaiian king was dead and so was annexation.

But there were successes in foreign policy under Pierce. Commodore Matthew C. Perry opened Japan to American trade in 1854. Disagreements between Great Britain and the United States over commercial fishing rights along the North American shores were settled by the Canadian Reciprocity Treaty in mid-1854. The treaty also eliminated import duties on certain goods traded between the United States and Canada.

A dispute between Great Britain and the United States over Central America— only a few years after the signing of the Clayton-Bulwer Treaty—threatened to result in war. The treaty had provided that neither country would ever "occupy, or fortify, or colonize, or assume or exercise any dominion over Nicaragua, Costa Rica, the Mosquito Coast [east coast of Nicaragua and Honduras] or any part of Central America." But there was disagreement over whether that meant the British were to vacate their pretreaty holdings in the area— the Bay Islands, Greytown (Nicaragua), and the Mosquito Coast. There was also a dangerous moment when an American naval officer sent by Fillmore to protect American interests in Greytown captured that community in 1853. Two years later, Pierce did nothing to prevent a free-lance filibuster named William Walker from taking over civil-war-torn Nicaragua, in order to protect the interests there of an American firm, the Accessory Transit Company. The President issued a proclamation against the filibustering, but after refusing to receive one emissary from the Walker government, he decided to see the next in 1856, thus in effect recognizing the government. When Cornelius Vanderbilt, who took over control of the Accessory Transit Company, brought about Walker's downfall, the situation was relieved: Britain ceded, as free territories, the Bay Islands to Honduras, and Greytown and the Mosquito Coast to Nicaragua.

Pierce began to gather strength of purpose as the 1856 nominating convention approached; he wanted to stay in the White House. But "Bleeding Kansas" ruined him. He continued to stand by the principle of local sovereignty and the constitutional rights of the slave states in the slavery question, and he castigated the abolitionists as fanatics. As far as the North was concerned, he was anathema, and the Southern Democrats felt that his loss of strength in the North made him an unacceptable candidate for 1856. The convention nominated, instead, James Buchanan of Pennsylvania.

After he left office, he and Mrs. Pierce went to Europe for about two years. When they returned, they found that there was a movement to run him again for the Presidency. But by this time he wanted no part of it, and Pierce forbade his supporters to nominate him.

When the Democratic party fell apart in 1860 and Abraham Lincoln won the election for an obviously sectional party, Pierce was dismayed. Dismay became bitter opposition to Lincoln during the Civil War. Pierce was sharply criticized for his position by his neighbors; the most crushing blow to his reputation came on July 4, 1863, when he spoke at a Democratic rally in Concord. He condemned this "fearful, fruitless, fatal Civil War." That afternoon, while the meeting went on, news circulated through the crowd of a great Northern victory at Gettysburg.

Two further blows followed. His wife died at the end of that year. The next spring, he and Hawthorne went off together on a trip to the White Mountains—an attempt to restore the writer's health. But Hawthorne died one night in a bedroom adjoining Pierce's. At Hawthorne's funeral the former President was pointedly snubbed by the New England literati and was not included among the pallbearers. A broken man, Pierce himself died on October 8, 1869.

"I can not . . . bow to the storm," he had written his wife shortly before her death. And he did not. But like a stiff and brittle tree he had been shattered by the hurricane.

—MARTIN LURAY

Franklin Pierce

A PICTURE PORTFOLIO

The Democrats were the party of compromise in 1852, and to adorn their campaign banners they chose two moderates—one a Yankee, the other a Southerner.

Franklin Pierce, shown (at right) on a commemorative medal, was, at forty-eight, the youngest President yet inaugurated. He was also one of the best looking (he was nicknamed Handsome Frank) and most charming: "Courtly and polished," one senator's wife described him. Mrs. Jefferson Davis noted that Pierce scolded so gently "the sting was all taken out." And his good manners were not saved just for influential Washingtonians. The President "gives me the compliments of the morning," testified the White House doorkeeper, "as grandly as he does General Scott."

GAS AND GLORY.

Nathaniel Hawthorne spoke in awed tones of Pierce's good luck, but in the Mexican War, Brigadier General Pierce was anything but fortunate. At the start of his first major action, outside Mexico City, his horse—startled by exploding shells—bucked and tossed him forward so that the pommel of his saddle was driven into his groin. He fainted; the horse fell, broke its leg, and tore Pierce's knee. In the confusion an officer shouted that the unconscious Pierce was a coward—a report that spread. Despite his injuries and intestinal infections, Pierce kept forcing himself into action during the rest of the campaign, but he never managed to find the opportunity for heroic redemption of his reputation—as the uncomplimentary cartoon above indicates.

WINFIELD SCOTT

AN UNEXPECTED VICTOR

When the 1852 Democratic convention, after laboring long, gave birth to a dark horse from New Hampshire, Senator Stephen A. Douglas commented dryly, "Hereafter, no private citizen is safe." For the dark horse, Franklin Pierce, it was a breath-taking turnabout. He had risen rapidly and had become a United States senator in 1837, at the age of thirty-three; but his wife hated Washington, and after only one term he had exchanged a career in national politics for a Granite State law practice. His subsequent service as a general in the Mexican War was undistinguished. In 1850, though Pierce was still leader of the New Hampshire Democratic party, he seemed about as far from the White House as from the moon. Yet by the time of the national convention, three factors had intervened: the Compromise of 1850 gave the nation hope for settlement of the slavery issue; Pierce successfully fought disruptive free-soil infiltration of the state party during the 1851 gubernatorial campaign, thus earning favorable notice nationally; and the leading contenders for the Democratic presidential nomination proved strong enough only to block each other. A deadlock breaker—someone acceptable to the South—was needed, and Pierce was chosen on the forty-ninth ballot. His electoral vote margin in the election that fall, 254 to 42, was the largest since that of James Monroe in 1820.

Andrew Jackson had called him a "hectoring bully," and Polk termed him "visionary," but in the eyes of the nation General Winfield Scott was nothing less than a hero when the Whigs offered him the presidential nomination in 1852. Publicly acclaimed for his courage at Chippewa and Lundy's Lane in the War of 1812, he was brevetted a major general. He fought in the Black Hawk War, and when, in 1837, Jackson ordered an inquiry into General Scott's handling of the Creek and Seminole campaigns, the court praised the soldier's "energy, steadiness, and ability." His accomplishments as peacemaker in 1838 and 1839 were no less impressive. In little more than a year, he restored peace along the Canadian border; pacified some sixteen thousand dispossessed Cherokee; and averted a war with Great Britain in the Maine boundary dispute. As general in chief of the Army during the Mexican War, he led the victorious assault on the enemy capital and again won public applause. National sentiment was not strong enough, however, to make him President, and in the election of 1852 he was roundly defeated by Pierce. Resuming his military duties, he averted a serious conflict with Great Britain in 1859 over possession of San Juan Island off the Pacific coast. During the Civil War, he remained loyal to the Union, serving briefly as general in chief. He retired in 1861 and died five years later, at eighty.

EXPANSION

America at mid-cen-
tury was expansion minded, seeking more
trade abroad, more land on the American
continent. Pierce planned to encourage the
nation's growth as a world power, and he
succeeded, to some extent, with the help of
his able Secretary of State, William L.

*Commodore Matthew C. Perry, shown above in a portrait
by a Japanese artist, was sent by President Fillmore to
open isolationist Japan to American trade; during
Pierce's term, Perry succeeded in negotiating a treaty.
Below is a Japanese depiction of one of the black side-
wheeler warships under Commodore Perry's command.*

Marcy. They completed a record number of treaties for a four-year administration, including the Gadsden Purchase, the Canadian Reciprocity Treaty (which involved North Atlantic fishing rights and commerce between the United States and Canada), and trade treaties with the Netherlands and Denmark. They sent a consul general to Japan to follow up Commodore Perry's success there. But their attempt to attach Cuba to the United States came to naught. The blustering tone of the Ostend Manifesto and the filibustering of William Walker in Central America epitomized a problem that Pierce did little to solve: America's enthusiasm for expansion was giving the country a black eye overseas. Muttered a British diplomat, "These Yankees are . . . totally unscrupulous and dishonest and determined somehow or other to carry their Point."

The painting above by Albert J. Fountain, Jr., depicts the July 4, 1854, celebration of the Gadsden Purchase in Mesilla, New Mexico Territory. The land (now southern Arizona and New Mexico) was bought at the urging of Pierce's Secretary of War, Jefferson Davis, to clear the way for a transcontinental railroad across the South.

WIELDERS OF THE PEN

BOTH: CULVER PICTURES

NATHANIEL HAWTHORNE

"I used to think," wrote Nathaniel Hawthorne, that "I could imagine all passions, all feelings, and states of heart and mind." Born in Salem, Massachusetts, of Puritan stock, Hawthorne's young imagination was nurtured by wide and varied reading. In 1821 he entered Bowdoin College, where he established an intimate and lasting friendship with a fellow student, future President Franklin Pierce. Returning to Salem after graduation, he spent the next twelve years in seclusion until, in 1837, he published his first important work, the *Twice-Told Tales*. After a brief association with the transcendentalists at Brook Farm, he moved to Concord in 1842, where he cultivated the friendship of Thoreau. In 1850 he published his most famous novel, *The Scarlet Letter*, which dealt with the moral decay of seventeenth-century Puritanism. The next year he published *The House of the Seven Gables*, again concerned with decadent New England, and in 1852, *The Blithedale Romance*, based on his experiences at Brook Farm. Upon Pierce's nomination in 1852, he published a campaign biography, *The Life of Franklin Pierce*, and was rewarded with an appointment as U.S. consul at Liverpool. Four years after his return from Europe in 1860, he died while traveling through New England with Pierce.

HENRY DAVID THOREAU

"Walden was, in fact, to Thoreau," wrote an early biographer, "what Brook Farm was to others of the transcendentalists—a retreat suitable for philosophic meditation, and the practice of a simpler, hardier, and healthier life." Graduating from Harvard in 1837, Henry David Thoreau became acquainted with the transcendentalists in the home of Emerson, where he lived from 1841 to 1843. In 1845 he commenced two years of seclusion at Walden Pond, gathering material for his famous social critique, *Walden, or Life in the Woods*, published in 1854. Thoreau was arrested when, as a gesture of protest against slavery and the Mexican War, he refused to pay a state poll tax. His subsequent essay, *Civil Disobedience*, defended the theory of passive resistance. Returning to his home in Concord, Massachusetts, he worked on the completion of his loosely strung narrative *A Week on the Concord and Merrimack Rivers*, published in 1849. As a lecturer during the 1850's, he became increasingly concerned with the slavery question; and when John Brown was arrested after his raid at Harpers Ferry in 1859, Thoreau was one of the first and most enthusiastic to speak in the abolitionist's defense. After his death in 1862, the voluminous journals Thoreau kept throughout his life were published.

RALPH WALDO EMERSON

Ralph Waldo Emerson—poet, essayist, and philosopher—was born in Boston, Massachusetts, in 1803, graduated from Harvard in 1821, and entered the Unitarian ministry in 1826. Breaking with the church on a question of dogma, he left for a tour of Europe in 1832. His fortunate meetings with Coleridge, Carlyle, and Wordsworth, and their discussions of the doctrines of German idealism, influenced his own philosophy in the direction of transcendentalism. Upon his return, he expounded his new theories from the lecture platform and in his first book, *Nature*, published in 1836. In the same year, he helped to form the Transcendental Club. His lectures, published in 1841 and 1844 as *Essays*, brought him international recognition; and his reputation as a poet was established with his first volume of poems in 1847 and a second volume published twenty years later. During the 1850's, he spoke out against the injustices of slavery, defending the position of John Brown and the abolitionists. His friends included Longfellow, Hawthorne, Holmes, and other members of the Saturday Club, which he established. Throughout his life, Emerson kept a record of his thoughts and observations in his *Journals*; and these and other works were published after the author's death in 1882.

HARRIET BEECHER STOWE

"So you're the little woman who wrote the book that made this great war," said Lincoln to Harriet Beecher Stowe in 1863. Born in Connecticut in 1811, Harriet Elizabeth Beecher moved to Cincinnati in 1832, married a theology professor, Calvin E. Stowe, and returned to New England in 1850 when her husband took an appointment at Bowdoin College. Shortly thereafter, Mrs. Stowe began work on the novel that was to bring her international fame. Stirred to indignation by the passage of the Fugitive Slave Law in 1850, she heeded her sister-in-law's prompting to "write something that would make this whole nation feel what an accursed thing slavery is." *Uncle Tom's Cabin, or Life Among the Lowly* was completed in 1851. Within a year, 300,000 copies were sold; pirated editions were widely circulated abroad; and it became one of the most popular and controversial plays on the American stage. The mild-mannered, diminutive woman had kindled a violent dispute that would end only on the battlefields of the Civil War. In 1856 she published a second antislavery novel, *Dred, A Tale of the Great Dismal Swamp*. Remembered chiefly for her sympathetic characterization of the slave Uncle Tom, Mrs. Stowe was a prolific writer whose works fill sixteen volumes.

"BLEEDING KANSAS"

Kansas was the shoal on which the Pierce administration came to grief. Senator Stephen A. Douglas, ardent nationalist, would-be President, and investor in lands around Chicago, had been trying to get the Great Plains territorialized so that a transcontinental railroad might be built, using Chicago as one terminus. The South had its own proposed route and was not interested. So when a bill to organize the plains region was introduced in 1854, Douglas' Senate Committee on Territories tried to sweeten it a bit for the slavery interests, and the result was explosive—a bill creating the territories of Kansas and Nebraska and repealing the Missouri Compromise, thus opening all the Northern territories to slavery. Pierce was reportedly furious but because he needed Southern support for anything he might want to do in the future, he backed the bill. Kansas was soon the setting for a wild war over land and slavery and quickly became an explosive national issue. As his party began to crumble under the stresses this created, Pierce found himself to be the object of abuse from many sides.

The uproar caused by Kansas was unprecedented in its ferocity. The atmosphere in Congress was highly charged with epithets, threats, and violence. Senator Charles Sumner, reformer and abolitionist from Massachusetts, was, for one, a wellspring of vitriol. As he viciously attacked Stephen Douglas and the absent Andrew P. Butler of South Carolina in an 1856 debate over Kansas, Douglas remarked, "That damn fool will get himself killed by some other damn fool." He was not far wrong. Two days later, Senator Butler's nephew, Representative Preston Brooks, caught Sumner at his Senate desk and caned him into insensibility (above). With the family honor thus peculiarly satisfied, and with Sumner incapacitated for, as it turned out, three years, Brooks was censured by the House and resigned; he was re-elected—a triumph for sectional rancor.

The bitter cartoon at left blames the administration Democrats for the excesses of the proslavery forces in "Bleeding Kansas," while conveniently ignoring the excesses of antislavery Kansans. Secretary of State William L. Marcy and the Democrats' 1856 presidential nominee, James Buchanan, are shown stealing a corpse's belongings. Pierce, whose weakness for alcohol was often used against him, and Lewis Cass terrorize Miss Liberty, as Douglas gaily scalps a victim.

FACTS IN SUMMARY: FRANKLIN PIERCE

CHRONOLOGY

UNITED STATES		PIERCE
Jefferson re-elected President	1804	*Born November 23*
Madison elected President	1808	
War with England	1812	
Missouri Compromise	1820	
Monroe Doctrine	1823	
	1824	*Graduates from Bowdoin College*
	1827	*Admitted to the bar*
Jackson elected President	1828	
	1829	*Named to the New Hampshire legislature*
	1831	*Chosen speaker of the state legislature*
Jackson vetoes bill to recharter Bank of the U.S.	1832	
	1833	*Begins term in U.S. House of Representatives*
Rise of Whig party	1834	*Marries Jane Means Appleton*
		Nominated for second term in Congress
Siege of the Alamo	1836	*Elected to U.S. Senate*
Van Buren elected President		
Harrison elected President	1840	

UNITED STATES		PIERCE
Webster-Ashburton Treaty	1842	*Resigns from Senate*
War declared on Mexico	1846	*Declines to serve as U.S. Attorney General*
	1847	*Commissioned brigadier general of volunteers*
		Marches to Mexico City with Winfield Scott's expedition
Treaty of Guadalupe Hidalgo	1848	*Resigns from Army*
Compromise of 1850	1850	*Elected president of N.H. constitutional convention*
	1852	*Elected President*
Gadsden Purchase	1853	
Perry opens Japan to American trade	1854	*Signs Kansas-Nebraska Act*
Kansas-Nebraska Act		
Canadian Reciprocity Treaty		
Birth of Republican party		
Ostend Manifesto		
	1855	*Issues proclamation against William Walker's invasion of Nicaragua*
Civil war in Kansas	1856	
Buchanan elected President		
Dred Scott decision	1857	*Travels to Europe*

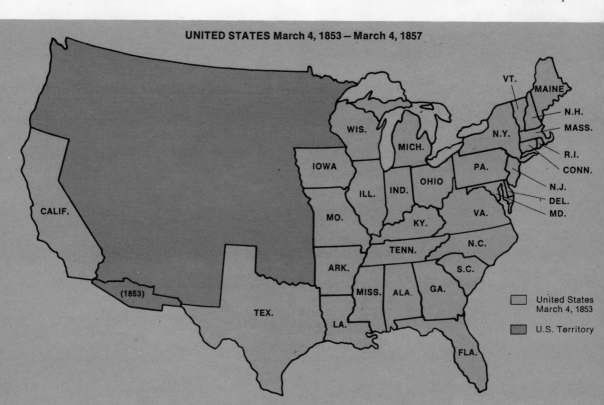

UNITED STATES March 4, 1853 — March 4, 1857

☐ United States March 4, 1853

■ U.S. Territory

This view of Bowdoin College in Maine was painted in 1821, three years before Pierce graduated.

Lincoln-Douglas debates	1858	
John Brown's raid	1859	*Returns to United States*
Lincoln elected President	1860	
Civil War begins	1861	
	1863	*Jane Pierce dies*
Lincoln assassinated	1865	
Johnson becomes President		
~~ant~~ elected President	1868	
	1869	*Dies October 8*

BIOGRAPHICAL FACTS

BIRTH: Hillsboro, N.H., Nov. 23, 1804

ANCESTRY: English

FATHER: Benjamin Pierce; b. Chelmsford, Mass., Dec. 25, 1757; d. April 1, 1839

FATHER'S OCCUPATIONS: Soldier; farmer; governor of New Hampshire

MOTHER: Anna Kendrick Pierce; b. 1768; d. Dec., 1838

BROTHERS: Benjamin Kendrick (1790–1850); John Sullivan (1796–1824); Charles Grandison (1803–1828); Henry Dearborn (1812–1880)

SISTERS: Nancy M. (1792–1837); Harriet B. (1800–1837)

HALF SISTER: Elizabeth Andrews (1788–1855)

WIFE: Jane Means Appleton; b. Hampton, N.H., March 12, 1806; d. Andover, Mass., Dec. 2, 1863

MARRIAGE: Amherst, N.H., Nov. 19, 1834

CHILDREN: Frank Robert (1839–1843); Benjamin (1841–1853)

HOME: Pierce Homestead, Hillsboro Upper Village, N.H.

EDUCATION: Attended public school and Hancock Academy; graduated from Bowdoin College (1824)

RELIGIOUS AFFILIATION: Episcopalian

OCCUPATIONS BEFORE PRESIDENCY: Lawyer; politician; soldier

MILITARY SERVICE: Brigadier general in U.S. Army (1847–1848)

PRE-PRESIDENTIAL OFFICES: Member and Speaker of N.H. Legislature; Member of U.S. House of Representatives; Member of U.S. Senate; President of N.H. Constitutional Convention

POLITICAL PARTY: Democratic

AGE AT INAUGURATION: 48

OCCUPATION AFTER PRESIDENCY: Retired

DEATH: Concord, N.H., Oct. 8, 1869

PLACE OF BURIAL: Old North Cemetery, Concord, N.H.

ELECTION OF 1852

CANDIDATES	ELECTORAL VOTE	POPULAR VOTE
Franklin Pierce Democratic	254	1,601,117
Winfield Scott Whig	42	1,385,453
John P. Hale Free-Soil	—	155,825

THE PIERCE ADMINISTRATION

INAUGURATION: March 4, 1853; the Capitol, Washington, D.C.

VICE PRESIDENT: William R. King (died April 18, 1853)

SECRETARY OF STATE: William L. Marcy

SECRETARY OF THE TREASURY: James Guthrie

SECRETARY OF WAR: Jefferson Davis

ATTORNEY GENERAL: Caleb Cushing

POSTMASTER GENERAL: James Campbell

SECRETARY OF THE NAVY: James C. Dobbin

SECRETARY OF THE INTERIOR: Robert McClelland

SUPREME COURT APPOINTMENT: John A. Campbell (1853)

33rd CONGRESS (March 4, 1853–March 4, 1855):
Senate: 38 Democrats; 22 Whigs; 2 Others
House: 159 Democrats; 71 Whigs; 4 Others

34th CONGRESS (March 4, 1855–March 4, 1857):
Senate: 40 Democrats; 15 Republicans; 5 Others
House: 108 Republicans; 83 Democrats; 43 Others

END OF PRESIDENTIAL TERM: March 4, 1857

JAMES BUCHANAN

James Buchanan was the last in a string of Presidents, Northern men with Southern principles or vice versa, who stood for compromise between two bitterly opposed groups of radicals; the last in a line chosen because, it was thought, they would not press for a nation-splitting decision on the slavery issue. During their service, the situation had grown more dangerous despite continued legal and political compromises. Pierce had been broken by it. Now it was Buchanan's turn.

When he assumed the Presidency, this son of a Pennsylvania storekeeper had been in public life for more than forty years. Born April 23, 1791, near Mercersburg, Pennsylvania, he was graduated from Dickinson College in 1809 and began the practice of law three years later. He became a Federalist state legislator in Pennsylvania in 1814 and a member of Congress in 1821.

Buchanan was a gentle, diplomatic person, religiously fatalistic in his approach to life. He stood six feet tall and was a heavy man, but because his sight was uneven (one eye being nearsighted, the other farsighted), he cocked his head down and to one side when addressing or listening to someone, giving the impression of shyness and humility. Considered charming and good-looking, he nevertheless remained a bachelor all his life. He came closest to the altar when he was in his late twenties, but his devotion to work got in the way of his courting, and misunderstandings followed; his fiancée, Ann Coleman, broke off the engagement. Because Ann was a wealthy girl, and because her parents had felt all along that Buchanan was marrying her for her money, he was afraid that protestations of love would be suspect. So he did not offer them. Ann died soon afterward, apparently as a result of a hysterical fit. Buchanan's role in the tragedy was characteristic; he considered all the angles and was not ruled by his emotions. Success came to him in politics because he

The portrait of James Buchanan is by G. P. A. Healy.

played it like a game of chess—cautiously, step by step. He habitually kept his financial records accurate to the penny and knew how every cent was spent; before long he had amassed a considerable fortune. With similar care he observed and took advantage of the constantly shifting schisms in politics and eased his way upward through the maze. After ten years' service in Congress, during which he left the moribund Federalists for the Jacksonian Democrats, he went to Russia as United States minister in 1832. He was elected to the Senate in 1834 and was re-elected twice. Not a moving speaker as either a lawyer or a legislator, he was a conscientious committee member and was meticulously detailed when presenting a case. Contemporaries found his plodding caution irritating—but worthy of respect nonetheless.

By 1844 he had become a possibility for the Presidency. He lost the Democratic nomination to Polk that year, then worked hard to bring Pennsylvania into the Democratic column; as a result he was awarded the post of Secretary of State. Buchanan and Polk respected each other, but they battled constantly during the next four years. Polk had made all his Cabinet members promise that they would not actively seek the presidential nomination of 1848, but Buchanan had taken the post for the prestige it would bring him, and he competed with Polk for leadership and laurels in foreign policy. "If I would yield up the government into his hands," wrote Polk, "and suffer him to be in effect President . . . I have no doubt he would be cheerful and satisfied." Toward the end of his term in the State Department, Buchanan began to campaign quietly for votes at the convention. But he lost to Lewis Cass of Michigan and retired to a new estate, "Wheatland," outside Lancaster. Then the maneuvering for the presidential nomination began again, and failed again in 1852, as Franklin Pierce won on the forty-ninth ballot.

In the spring of 1853, President Pierce convinced Buchanan to represent him in Great Britain. Although his ministry was not a great success—he became involved in the controversial Ostend Manifesto—his absence from the country during Pierce's administration proved fortunate: he was not a participant in the Kansas-Nebraska debate and, therefore, had no responsibility for "Bleeding Kansas."

Kansas, and the larger question of slavery in the United States, were to be the major issues of the 1856 campaign. Buchanan was known as a conservative, a compromise man. "I am not friendly to slavery in the abstract . . ." he had said, "[but] the rights of the south, under our constitutional compact, are as much entitled to protection as those of any other portion of the Union." Consistently he had held to the view that the abolitionists should be quiet and that everyone should show forbearance toward one another. This position was popular with the South and with Unionists in the North; Buchanan, a Northerner, thus fitted into the category from which the Democrats had been selecting their nominees.

After he returned from England, Buchanan began to emerge as the leading candidate because, unlike President Pierce and Senator Stephen A. Douglas, he had made no enemies over Kansas, which divided the Democrats as it did the country as a whole. After twelve ballots at the convention, Pierce was out of the running. Douglas withdrew after four more, and Buchanan was nominated by acclamation.

In November he polled less than half the popular vote, but won in the electoral college, 174 votes to 114 for the Republican, John C. Frémont, and 8 for the Know-Nothing, Millard Fillmore. Ominously, though Buchanan won New Jersey, Pennsylvania, Indiana, Illinois, and California, the bulk of his strength lay in the South. The Republican party, in its first major test, had swept the Northeast.

Thus, Buchanan came into the office of President as a contradiction: the Unionist elected without the votes of one of the contending sections. He saw the danger: "The great object of my administration," he wrote, "will be to arrest, if possible, the agitation of the slavery question at the North, and to destroy sectional parties."

The Kansas issue was the first crucial problem he had to meet, and for a while he did so with determination. Before he was inaugurated he suggested to friends on the Supreme Court that the Dred Scott case, then under consideration, be used as a platform for defining Congress' role in the slavery question. Scott was a slave who had been taken from Missouri into Wisconsin Territory and Illinois during the 1830's by his master, an Army doctor. Scott eventually sued in Missouri for his freedom on the grounds that his temporary removal to a free area had automatically given him the right to be free. Shortly after Buchanan entered office, the Court announced its decision: Scott was a slave, not a citizen, and thus could not sue for anything; and because the Missouri Compromise had forbidden slavery north of the Mason-Dixon Line, it had deprived Southern slaveowners of the right to take their property wherever they wished and had therefore been unconstitutional. Congress, the Court said, could not legislate concerning slavery in a territory, and this implied that neither could any territory created by Congress. All territories were open to slavery and could exclude slavery only when they became states.

Buchanan had had a considerable effect on the Court's pronouncement. Not only had he suggested elaboration of the decision, but he had put pressure on an associate justice from Pennsylvania, Robert C. Grier, to support it. He hoped that this would settle the Kansas controversy, but it did the opposite, increasing the anger in the North against the South.

To cope with the immediate situation in Kansas, Buchanan selected Robert J. Walker of Mississippi to be territorial governor and to oversee the territory's progress toward statehood. The best choice yet for that position, Walker was a levelheaded, no-nonsense Unionist. But even he was not able to bring order out of the chaos.

Sooner or later Kansas was going to become a free state. Douglas had thought so;

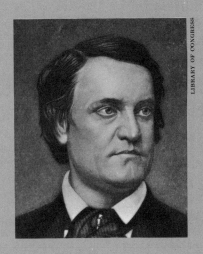

JOHN C. BRECKINRIDGE

Because the Democrats needed a Southern candidate to balance their ticket in 1856, thirty-five-year-old John C. Breckinridge of Kentucky was nominated for the Vice Presidency. Breckinridge had entered politics through the Kentucky legislature in 1849, was elected to Congress in 1851, and was soon one of the party's most prominent members. As Buchanan's Vice President from 1857 to 1861, he strove to maintain order in a divided Senate, advocating adoption of the Crittenden Compromise as a solution to the bitter slavery conflict between North and South. In 1860 he was nominated for President by the Southern wing of the badly split Democratic party. Opposing Douglas of the Northern Democrats and Lincoln of the Republicans, he defended himself against charges of promoting disunion, maintaining that he "never did an act nor cherished a thought that was not full of devotion to the Constitution and the Union." After Lincoln's election, Breckinridge represented his state in the Senate, defending her neutral position in the Civil War. When Kentucky later befriended the Union, however, Breckinridge joined the Confederate army and was expelled from the Senate as a traitor. In 1865 he was made Confederate secretary of war, escaping to Europe after Lee's surrender. In 1869 the federal government permitted him to return to Lexington, where he died in 1875.

so had Pierce; so did Buchanan. The odds were strongly against the proslavery men; they were already outnumbered in the territory by about four to one. Any fair process of producing a state constitution would result in a prohibition of slavery. However, early in 1857 the proslavery faction ran the government recognized as official in Washington and could control the election of delegates to a constitutional convention. When voter registration for that election began, the Free-Soilers assisted their opponents by refusing to register; they wanted nothing to do with the Lecompton (proslavery) government and hoped to discredit it by making the election appear unfair. As a result, proslavery delegates were elected. Then elections to the territorial legislature were held; for the first time the two factions contested for seats in the same legislature. When Walker discovered and threw out fraudulent returns from two areas, the antislavery party won a majority. Walker's action caused an uproar in the South. In that atmosphere the constitutional convention met at Lecompton. It is generally agreed that the delegates were a motley crowd of roughnecks, unequipped to write a constitution that would calm the situation. Furthermore, they were under pressure from the South not to submit their product to the people of the territory for approval. When they finished, they had decided to present only one question to popular vote: Should more slaves be allowed into Kansas?

In the constitution, they had provided that Kansas slaveowners could keep the approximately two hundred slaves then in Kansas if slavery were voted down. This "abolition" clause was similar to property-protection measures taken earlier by various Northern states when they outlawed slavery. But under the circumstances it was like waving a red flag. The Republicans blew it up out of all proportion. Considering, in addition, that the whole constitution was not to be submitted to a vote, and that it specified that no amendments were to be made until 1864, the proponents of slavery did appear to be engaging in trickery.

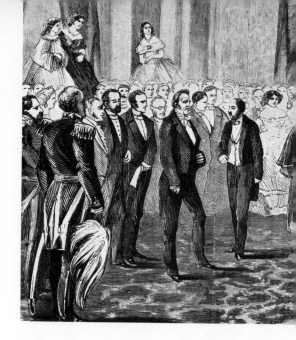

For months Buchanan had vacillated between calling for a referendum only on slavery or for one on the entire constitution. Finally he had promised Governor Walker he would support the latter course. But when the results of the territorial election and the Lecompton convention were received in Washington, Buchanan's Southern advisers, armed with threats of secession from several slave states, convinced him to change his mind again. He concluded that although the Lecompton measures would cause some trouble, they were, after all, legal, and that establishing Kansas as a state—any kind of a state—would end the national quarrel over the territory.

Senator Douglas, who had assured everyone during the Kansas-Nebraska debate that Kansas would enter the Union as a free state as the result of a popular vote, saw the actions of the Lecompton body as a violation of the popular-sovereignty principle. Moreover, he was up for re-election in Illinois, where the Lecompton government was thoroughly disliked. If he backed Buchanan's decision, he would lose, and his chances for the Presidency in 1860 would be diminished. He hurried to the White House to talk to the President. At the end of an angry conference, he told Buchanan he would have to oppose the administration if it allowed the Lecompton constitution to come to Congress without a vote on the en-

At left, Buchanan receives the first Japanese ambassadors to the United States, in May, 1860. Above is one of the Japanese gifts, "The Emperor's Bowl," the largest known porcelain in the world.

tire paper by the inhabitants of the territory. Buchanan, in turn, warned Douglas against fighting the administration and reminded him of how Andrew Jackson had ruined Democrats who opposed him. "Mr. President," said Douglas. "I wish you to remember that General Jackson is dead!"

In his annual message, delivered less than a week after Douglas broke with him, Buchanan told Congress he would send it the Lecompton constitution following the "with-slavery, without-slavery" vote. Within two weeks, in a referendum held under the aegis of the Lecompton convention, Kansas voted 6,226 to 569 for the constitution with slavery. Then the new Free-Soil legislature in the territory called for another vote and offered the whole constitution, as well as the slavery question, for the approval of the voters. The constitution was disapproved 10,226 to 162. Even so, Buchanan sent the constitution to Congress in February, 1858, and advised that Kansas be admitted. The debate that followed was long and bitter. But on April 1, 1858, Douglas Democrats, Republicans, and Know-Nothings combined to prevent passage of the Lecompton instrument in the House. Kansas would not become a state, as it turned out, until 1861.

A disastrous step had been taken toward war. Buchanan had given way to pressure from the South. Certainly, anything he did at the time was bound to stir up bitterness.

But the Southern extremists, who were encouraged by their success with him and enraged by the defeat of the Lecompton constitution in Congress, grew more clamorous.

Other forces were at work to aid them. In August, 1857, a business panic broke out in the North. To the South, aroused by religious revivalism and the denominational schisms reflecting the slavery controversy, the financial ruin in the North seemed a just retribution for the abolition movement and for the cluttered, seamy life of the cities. In the 1840's, Ralph Waldo Emerson had written, "Cotton thread holds the Union together. . . ." But the South was barely troubled by the Panic of 1857, and it began to feel that the North needed *it* far more than vice versa; Southern society was stable, Northern society was corrupt and at the mercy of financiers. If the North did not conform to Southern wishes, the South would break the thread of the Union and flourish.

More dramatic, and just as important, was an incident at a small town in Virginia in the fall of 1859. With a handful of whites and Negroes, a madman named John Brown, who had led a massacre in Kansas in 1856, seized the federal arsenal and a rifle factory at Harpers Ferry. He intended to start a Negro insurrection. Although he failed— federal troops soon captured Brown, who was tried and hanged—he became in both North and South a symbol of noncompromise. Even Southern moderates began to feel forced to choose between the idea of Union and protection of a familiar way of life against a dangerous enemy.

Slavery was not the only issue of Buchanan's administration. Nor was Kansas the only territory that proved a problem for him. "Deseret," the Mormon promised land, established by the Compromise of 1850 as the Territory of Utah, had been treated as an ill-favored stepchild for several years. Its applications for statehood had been ignored, and in 1855 Pierce had made three federal judiciary appointments for the territory that were remarkable for their inappropriateness: all three men were enemies of the Mormon community. The judges were unable to exercise much authority in the territory, mainly because the inhabitants ignored them; so in 1857 they came east to complain. Buchanan named a new governor, Alfred Cumming, to replace Brigham Young and ordered west a 2,500-man army to help sustain the law. Lack of communications from Washington left the Mormons with the impression they were being invaded. The Mormon War began, highlighted by severe harassment of the approaching troops and a massacre of Californian emigrants by Mormons and Indians. At last, Thomas L. Kane of Philadelphia, a friend of Buchanan's and a Mormon sympathizer, suggested that he be sent to Salt Lake City to talk to Young. Buchanan agreed, and gradually the matter was ironed out, with Cumming accepted as governor.

Foreign policy was always Buchanan's strong suit. Despite the restrictions imposed on him by the growing domestic crisis, it was in this area that he achieved his greatest successes as President. Using his diplomatic contacts in Great Britain, he developed with the British an interpretation of the troublesome Clayton-Bulwer Treaty—an attempt to guarantee nonintervention in Central America by the United States and Great Britain—that was satisfactory to both sides.

At the same time, the President labored to enlarge United States influence in Central and South America, partly as a step toward national expansion and partly because the constant political turmoil south of the border invited intervention by European powers. While discouraging filibustering, he brought American power to bear on—among others —Nicaragua (winning the right to protect routes across the isthmus with American arms) and Mexico (which agreed to let the United States send troops into the country whenever uprisings threatened the Mexican government). The Senate refused to ratify

"Picturesque and elegant," one visitor called Wheatland, Buchanan's home in Pennsylvania. Comfortably spacious and surrounded by wheat farms, its grounds were patrolled by a pair of large pinioned eagles.

these treaties, but had Buchanan been President in a quieter time, he might today be remembered as an empire builder.

From the beginning of his term Buchanan had to deal with a chaotic situation in Congress. Though the reigning Democrats were a national party in form—and the only one then remaining in American politics—they were not national in substance. They were divided along sectional lines—North versus South versus West. Washington was full of lobbyists for various enterprises, who had liquor to pour and money to spend. As sectionalism weakened party discipline, and rising Republican strength foreshadowed an 1860 defeat, Democratic congressmen tended to look after their private and local power rather than national needs, and failed to provide the President with the national "consensus" he so ardently desired. What small chance there was for party unity vanished in the Lecompton fight; this left the Douglas Democrats and the Southern extremists antagonistic to the administration and cost the party control of the Lower House after the mid-term elections.

Buchanan's legislative program, an ambitious one which included the purchase of Cuba and enlargement of the armed forces, was wrecked by sectionalist bickering and the vengefulness of congressmen who could not have their own way. Even ordinary appropriation bills, needed to keep the government in operation, had trouble passing.

Buchanan stood curiously disconnected from the realities. After seeing the dismaying returns in the mid-term elections, he could still make the amazing statement that "the prospects are daily brightening. From present appearances the party will ere long be thoroughly united." Yet every day the South drew further away from the ideal of the old Union. At odds with the North and West, trapped, as it felt, by the weight of increasing Northern population, frightened by the possibility of slave emancipation or insurrection, insulted and angered by William Lloyd Garrison, Harriet Beecher Stowe, and their kind, the South looked upon the North as a foreign government keeping it in

and, whatever the result may be, I shall carry to my grave the consciousness that I at least meant well for my country.

James Buchanan

In twenty-three words—at the close of a volume defending his Presidency—James Buchanan capsuled the tragedy of a good man out of his depth.

thrall and in danger. They saw Northern Democrats pulling out of line, as Douglas had done, and knew what this meant for 1860. The election of a President representing a purely Northern party—either William Seward or Abraham Lincoln—would be sufficient cause, all by itself, for setting up a Southern confederacy. Even before Lincoln's election, preparations were being made for that eventuality.

Buchanan had decided before his inauguration not to stand for re-election; he thought two terms were too long for any man to be President. The Democrats were unable to unify behind anyone else, and Lincoln won with much less than a popular majority. On the morning after the election, the federal district judge in South Carolina resigned his post and other representatives of the national government there did the same.

The calls for secession were growing louder in Georgia, Alabama, Mississippi, Louisiana, and Florida, but South Carolina, the old home of nullification, presented the most immediate danger to the Union. Because there was talk of the possible capture of the forts in Charleston Harbor by the secessionists, Colonel John L. Gardner, commanding the garrison there, decided to remove federal arms from the arsenal in the middle of Charleston as a precaution. But his plans were stymied by an outraged mob.

Buchanan scolded the North for the abolition movement and begged the Southern states to wait and see what Lincoln did before they took any precipitous action. If the abolitionists continued to plague the South, or if Lincoln were to "invade" the constitutional rights of the slave states, he said, then a rebellion might be justified. On the other hand, secession was illegal. But the federal government had no means to prevent it or to suppress it once it occurred. The present administration had the right to protect federal functions and property within a state, Buchanan said, but only defensively. It could not act unless attacked. It could not declare war against a state. The government would stay in Charleston to guard the forts and collect tariffs. But otherwise the maintenance of federal responsibility in South Carolina was peculiarly hampered, Buchanan said, by the fact that a number of federal officers there had resigned. Thus, certain official functions, particularly those pertaining to the enforcement of federal law (including putting down a rebellion), could not be sustained by force because there were no law officers.

The appeal to reason had reached, at last, the nadir of its futility. Buchanan was every inch the high-minded gentleman. As a lame-duck President his position was already weak, and he made it weaker by his self-restricting legalism. He denied himself powers that other Presidents before him had felt able to use in like emergencies—notably Washington in the Whisky Rebellion and Jackson in the Nullification Crisis.

South Carolina seceded before Christmas, followed quickly by Mississippi, Florida, Alabama, Georgia, Louisiana, and Texas. A provisional Confederate government had been organized by February 9, 1861. All over the South federal forts and arsenals were captured. Buchanan believed that by law he was still powerless to act. Practically speaking, he had only a few hundred troops at his disposal should he decide to use arms. And if he used them, would not war be inevitable? He begged Congress to give the government new powers on the one hand and to create a legal solution to the crisis on the other. He felt that the best solution lay in a clarifying amendment to the Constitution that would guarantee slavery in the states that wanted it. With Congress refusing to act, he tried to remain in the middle, giving in to no one, but pacifying both sides until a solution could be worked out. Those Northerners who support the South "are almost literally between two fires," he had once told John Calhoun. "I desire to come between the factions as a daysman with one hand on the head of each, counselling peace," he said now. And after leaving office he told his niece, "I acted for some time as a break-water between the North and the South, both surging with all their force against me."

When he retired to Wheatland that March, he left the crisis intact for Lincoln to deal with. In many ways this was appropriate, for neither Lincoln nor his party had been willing to help Buchanan. But in short order he was made the scapegoat for the havoc that followed. He was unfairly accused of having been proslavery and of having helped the South to arm for war. His failure to act at once in November to cut off secession was also criticized—justly, if one also gives him credit for seeking to maintain not just the Union, but his idea of constitutional government as well.

He supported Lincoln and the war, saying that he would have done as Lincoln did, once Fort Sumter was fired on. Lincoln was not grateful; he needed someone to blame for the war and led off the attack on Buchanan—an attack that continues to this day. "It is one of those great national prosecutions," wrote Buchanan himself before he died in 1868, ". . . necessary to vindicate the character of the Government. . . ." The world, he said, had "forgotten the circumstances" and blamed his "supineness."

It was a mild—and characteristically aloof—observation. But his appeal to "the circumstances" cannot be ignored. The intersectional struggle had evaded real control by the executive branch ever since John Tyler had come to office in 1841. The conciliating James Buchanan reaped a whirlwind that had been decades in the making. His administration was a failure, yet in many aspects it was less his administration than that of the "irrepressible conflict."

—MICHAEL HARWOOD

James Buchanan

A PICTURE PORTFOLIO

*Above Buchanan's head on an 1856 campaign ribbon is
a rooster, then the symbol of the Democratic party.*

BOTH: NEW-YORK HISTORICAL SOCIETY

Buchanan was not alone in the North in his belief that law and good will could hold the crumbling Union together. His election campaign was, like his predecessor's, founded on that idea, as is shown in the advertisement at right, published by Buchanan's supporters in Connecticut. Nonetheless, Republican John C. Frémont swept New England and New York, while Buchanan won by taking the whole South.

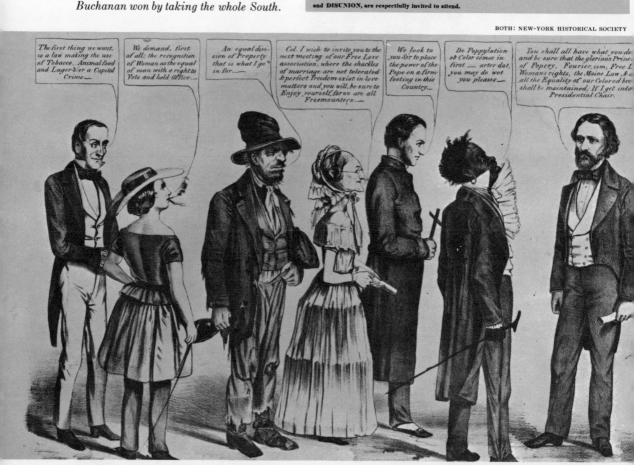

In many respects the new Republican party was the party of dissent and change. Louis Maurer's lithograph, done for Currier & Ives during the 1856 campaign, acidly makes this point, demonstrating that the Democrats, while preaching Union, were less than conciliatory toward a large segment of the electorate.

JOHN C. FRÉMONT

A MISCAST PRESIDENT

Buchanan inherited an exceedingly unsettled situation when the election of 1856 made him President. His nation was growing at a breath-taking pace; railroads, steamboats, and the telegraph were changing the age-old rhythm of human communication; the industrial revolution had come to America. Scientific thought and philosophy were being infiltrated by exciting, radical ideas; religion was in revivalist ferment; social institutions were being questioned, broken, remade. It was a time when much of the world had outlawed human slavery, but the United States remained half free, half slave. An increasingly large segment of its population, caught up in the spirit of change, angrily opposed the institution. Buchanan thought that the sectionalist clash thus precipitated was capable of reasonable, legal solution. Thus he believed that by winning a Supreme Court ruling—in the Dred Scott case—that delineated congressional powers over slavery in the territories, he had solved the problems of Kansas. Buchanan was emotionally isolated from the fervor that enveloped America. He had traveled little in the United States; he had seldom explored outside diplomacy, practical politics, and the law. He lacked both the experience and the temperament to fight the national fires with fire: not when they repeatedly flared up over Kansas, not when they wrecked his legislative program, not even when the South began its secession.

Explorer, soldier, and "Pathfinder" of the West, John C. Frémont was the first presidential candidate of the Republican party. Running against Buchanan on a free-soil platform, Frémont was chosen largely for his national prestige. His fame was linked to a series of important explorations—through South Pass in 1842 and to Oregon, the Sierra Nevada, and California in 1843 and 1844. An expedition on the eve of the Mexican War involved him in the conquest of California. His excessive zeal resulted in a court-martial, but made him a national hero. After a year as a United States senator and two more expeditions, he was adopted by the new party. "Free soil, free speech, and Frémont" was the Republican slogan, and among those distinguished citizens who supported him were Emerson, Bryant, and Longfellow. Support by the intellectuals and Northern abolitionists was insufficient, however, to counteract Unionist fears of Southern secession; and Frémont lost to the compromising Democratic candidate, Buchanan. When Civil War broke out, Frémont commanded the Department of the West, but his radical antislavery actions in Missouri led to his removal. Given a command in western Virginia, he soon resigned. In 1864 he was nominated for the Presidency by a group of Radical Republicans, but was persuaded to withdraw. Before his death in 1890, Frémont served for six years as the governor of Arizona Territory.

In the fall of 1859, John Brown (shown above in a modern painting by John Steuart Curry) led eighteen whites and Negroes in a raid on the arsenal and rifle factory at Harpers Ferry, Virginia, hoping to spark a slave rebellion. It did not work. Buchanan ordered in federal troops; Brown was captured and brought to trial. But the incident seemed to crystallize sectional antipathies, making President Buchanan's chosen role as compromiser more and more agonizing, increasingly untenable.

A SHAKY UNION

A Pictorial History of the Negro in America

There is a body of opinion in America, wrote New Hampshire abolitionist Nathaniel Rogers, which "abhors slavery in the abstract . . . but denies the right of any body or any thing to devise its overthrow, but slavery itself and slaveholders. It prays for the poor slave, that he might be elevated, while it stands both feet on his breast to keep him down." The description fitted Buchanan's views exactly. Admitting to a personal dislike of slavery, he nevertheless railed at abolitionists such as William Lloyd Garrison and John Brown for fomenting disunion. But, to his horror, the abolitionists did not want a union with slavery. As Garrison put it, *they*, at least, would not equivocate, and they would be heard.

As the above cartoon portrayed him, Buchanan was only a candle end, stubbornly flickering on despite fierce winds, while providing little light.

Frank Leslie's Illustrated Newspaper

"If it is deemed necessary that I should forfeit my life . . . and mingle my blood . . . with the blood of millions [of slaves]," Brown told his accusers, ". . . I say, let it be done." It was. On December 2, 1859, he was hanged at Charleston, and as the abolition hymn was soon to promise, John Brown's truth went marching on—to war.

DISCORDANT VOICES

FREDERICK DOUGLASS

Without the verification of history, the story of Frederick Douglass would seem to be an improbable piece of fiction. The son of a slave and an unknown white man, Douglass was reared in bondage in Maryland. Despite laws forbidding the education of slaves, he learned to read and write, increasing his fierce desire to be free. In 1838, at the age of twenty-one, he succeeded: he fled to New York, and then to New Bedford, Massachusetts, where he worked as a laborer and lived with the realization that his "runaway" status might be discovered at any time. His impressive physique and commanding voice soon made Douglass a spokesman for the state's antislavery society; in 1845 he daringly sharpened the sword hanging over his head by publishing his life story, *Narrative*. Two years later he arranged to buy his freedom and established a newspaper, the *North Star*, firmly setting his own policies despite conflicting advice from abolitionist friends. He lectured widely, advocated woman suffrage, and, during the war, recruited two Negro regiments, exhorting them, "Better even die than to live slaves. . . . The iron gate of our prison stands half open. One gallant rush . . . will fling it wide. . . ." During Reconstruction, he agitated for Negro civil rights, and by the time of his death in 1895, Douglass had held a number of federal offices, including that of minister to Haiti.

ROGER B. TANEY

Roger B. Taney's proslavery opinion in the Dred Scott case of 1857 should have surprised no one, for it was wholly in accord with the strict-constructionist, states' rights philosophy he had held since Jackson had appointed him Chief Justice of the Supreme Court in 1836. Groomed for politics in upper-class tidewater Maryland, Taney had been a Federalist state legislator early in the century but swung to Jackson in 1824; by 1831 he was Old Hickory's Attorney General. In 1834 the Senate refused to confirm him as Secretary of the Treasury, but not before Taney, who like Jackson saw the National Bank as a predator, had placed federal funds in "pet banks" while interim Secretary. Once installed on the high bench, Taney began to reverse the nationalist trends of his predecessor, John Marshall, by increasing the power of the states over corporations in the Charles River Bridge case and by construing the Constitution's commerce clause narrowly. Taney held that states should be free to act unless the Constitution specifically authorized federal intervention; a strong, Northern-dominated federal government, he felt, would stifle the South. Ironically, his Dred Scott decision speeded the South's downfall. During the war, Taney opposed President Lincoln's suspension of the writ of habeas corpus. Weak from recurrent illness, he died in 1864.

HENRY WARD BEECHER

Impulsive, dynamic Henry Ward Beecher was among the most influential antislavery spokesmen of mid-nineteenth-century America. With twenty-five hundred rapt listeners packing his Plymouth Church of Brooklyn each Sunday—and thousands more reading his words in pamphlets and newspapers— Beecher roundly condemned the Fugitive Slave Law, urged free-soilers to emigrate to Kansas (where their rifles were called Beecher's Bibles), and held mock auctions of Negro women to show the inhumanity of slavery. Ordained as a New School Presbyterian minister in 1838, Beecher preached for nine years in Indiana, where his intuitive, emotional, and optimistic concept of God, and his urge to reform injustices, were expounded in a natural, yet dramatically persuasive, oratorical style. During the Civil War, the brother of Harriet Beecher Stowe defended the Union cause before hostile British audiences and advocated emancipation. Beecher was a successful newspaper editor in the eighteen-sixties and seventies. He supported woman suffrage, and despite a long-held belief in miracles, embraced Darwinism. In 1875 he was cleared in a much-publicized adultery case, but the scandal, along with some of his unorthodox religious views, cast a shadow over his remaining years. In 1887 he died from a cerebral hemorrhage at the age of seventy-four.

CHARLES SUMNER

Charles Sumner, who considered himself "in morals, not politics," was a prewar abolitionist bellwether and a foe of moderate Reconstruction in those states that had committed the "suicide" of secession. Brilliant, vain, and unbending, Sumner was elected to the first of four Senate terms in 1851, despite violent conservative opposition in his native Boston. He bitterly denounced the Fugitive Slave Law, but his full rage was directed at the Kansas-Nebraska Act. Calling it a "swindle" and a "rape," he labeled Stephen Douglas a "noisome, squat and nameless animal" and was thrashed senseless in the Senate by a nephew of Senator Andrew Butler's (Sumner had excoriated Butler for embracing "the harlot, Slavery"). Badly injured, Sumner appeared rarely in the Senate for three years, but then resumed his vituperative antislavery speeches. In 1861 he helped avert an international crisis by urging Lincoln to free two Confederate diplomats who were removed from a British ship, the *Trent*. After the war, he insisted on immediate Negro suffrage and took part in the impeachment movement against Andrew Johnson. Sumner was sixty-three when he died in Washington in 1874. The implacable idealist once told Julia Ward Howe that he had lost interest in individuals. Mrs. Howe's prompt reply to Senator Sumner: "Why, Charles! God hasn't got as far as that yet."

These two cartoons sketch the ruin of a political career. Above, Douglas, whom Buchanan would not back for the 1860 nomination, crows about his victory, while Breckinridge is set in the ring as the Southern candidate. Below, Buchanan is portrayed as afraid to cope with South Carolina's demand for Fort Sumter.

THE HOUSE DIVIDED

The year 1860 was disastrous for the Democrats and the nation. Once the Democrats had paraded as the party of unity, but now, with the help of the titular leader, the party fell apart over the choice of a new President. Buchanan had long ago ruled himself out of the race and refused to reconsider. But Stephen A. Douglas as a Buchanan-supported candidate might, despite the inevitable Southern opposition, have held enough of the party together to sweep the middle states for the Democrats and beat Lincoln. But Buchanan's bitter fight with Douglas over slavery in the territories clouded his political judgment. He championed no one during the Democratic convention, and after the South bolted and nominated John Breckinridge, the President backed Breckinridge. He believed he might thereby help create an electoral vote deadlock that Congress would finally settle by choosing a moderate as Chief Executive. It was a case of too little, too late. With the Democrats in wild disarray, Lincoln won an electoral majority. Then, like a juggler who has suddenly lost control, Buchanan watched helplessly while everything fell in pieces around him. With the slave states, once his party's backbone, pulling out of the Union, capturing federal forts and arsenals all over the South, he held himself bound by law and lack of troops to do nothing but conciliate. He called despairingly for help from Congress, which was in no mood or condition to provide it, and from President-elect Lincoln, who did not think the situation as serious as Buchanan saw it and so (like the Republicans in Congress) found good political reasons for noncooperation and refused to support compromise measures. A sad Buchanan left the White House in 1861 having avoided war between the states, but only temporarily.

CHARLESTON

MERCURY

EXTRA:

Passed unanimously at 1.15 o'clock, P. M., December 20th, 1860.

AN ORDINANCE

To dissolve the Union between the State of South Carolina and other States united with her under the compact entitled "The Constitution of the United States of America."

We, the People of the State of South Carolina, in Convention assembled, do declare and ordain, and it is hereby declared and ordained,

That the Ordinance adopted by us in Convention, on the twenty-third day of May, in the year of our Lord one thousand seven hundred and eighty-eight, whereby the Constitution of the United States of America was ratified, and also, all Acts and parts of Acts of the General Assembly of this State, ratifying amendments of the said Constitution, are hereby repealed; and that the union now subsisting between South Carolina and other States, under the name of "The United States of America," is hereby dissolved.

THE

UNION

IS

DISSOLVED!

The news from Charleston presented Buchanan with a dilemma: secession was unconstitutional, but if a state seceded anyway, should it then be forced to return? If so, how? He never found the answers.

399

FACTS IN SUMMARY: JAMES BUCHANAN

CHRONOLOGY

UNITED STATES		BUCHANAN		UNITED STATES		BUCHANAN
	1791	*Born April 23*		Tyler becomes President	1841	
John Adams elected President	1796			Oregon boundary dispute	1844	*Defeated in bid for Democratic presidential nomination*
Jefferson elected President	1801			Polk elected President		
Madison elected President	1808			Annexation of Texas	1845	*Appointed Secretary of State*
	1809	*Graduates from Dickinson College*		Slidell mission to Mexico		*Declines Supreme Court appointment*
War of 1812	1812	*Admitted to the bar*		Oregon settlement	1846	*Negotiates Oregon Treaty with Great Britain*
Washington burned	1814	*Elected to Pennsylvania legislature*		War with Mexico		
Monroe elected President	1816	*Resumes law practice*		Gold discovered in California	1848	*Declines to run for governor of Pennsylvania*
Missouri Compromise	1820	*Elected to U.S. House of Representatives*		Taylor inaugurated as President	1849	
	1822	*Re-elected to U.S. House of Representatives*		Compromise of 1850	1850	*Opposes Compromise of 1850*
John Quincy Adams elected President	1825	*Begins third term in Congress*		Pierce elected President	1852	
Jackson elected President	1828			Gadsden Purchase	1853	*Appointed minister to Great Britain*
	1832	*Appointed minister to Russia*		Kansas-Nebraska Act	1854	*Participates in framing of Ostend Manifesto*
Rise of Whig party	1834	*Elected to U.S. Senate*		Civil war in Kansas	1856	*Elected President*
Siege of the Alamo	1836	*Re-elected to Senate*		Dred Scott decision	1857	*Upholds Lecompton convention in Kansas*
Van Buren elected President				Lecompton constitution rejected by Kansas	1858	*Submits Lecompton constitution to Congress*
Harrison elected President	1840			Lincoln-Douglas debates		
				John Brown's raid at Harpers Ferry	1859	*Opposes African slave trade*

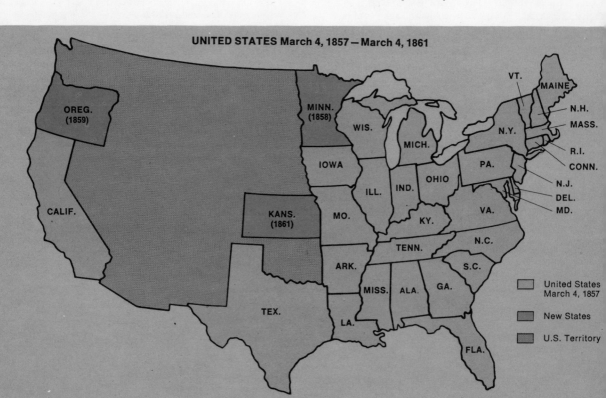

UNITED STATES March 4, 1857 — March 4, 1861

VT.
MAINE
N.H.
MASS.
R.I.
CONN.
N.J.
DEL.
MD.

OREG. (1859)
MINN. (1858)
WIS.
MICH.
N.Y.
PA.
VA.

IOWA
OHIO
ILL.
IND.
CALIF.
KANS. (1861)
MO.
KY.
N.C.
TENN.
S.C.
ARK.
ALA.
GA.
MISS.
TEX.
LA.
FLA.

United States March 4, 1857
New States
U.S. Territory

Lincoln elected President	1860	*Supports Crittenden resolution*
ᵘuth Carolina secedes		
Crittenden resolution		
ᵒvisional government formed by eleven seceding states	1861	*Submits Virginia Resolutions to Congress* *Retires to Wheatland*
Lincoln inaugurated as President		
Fort Sumter fired upon		
Civil War begins		
Battle of Gettysburg	1863	
Lee surrenders at Appomattox	1865	
Lincoln assassinated		
Andrew Johnson impeached	1868	*Dies June 1*

ᴵOGRAPHICAL FACTS

ᴿTH: Cove Gap, Pa., April 23, 1791

ᴺCESTRY: Scotch-Irish

ᴬTHER: James Buchanan; b. County Donegal, Ireland,
ᵘ61; d. Mercersburg, Pa., June 11, 1821

ᴬTHER'S OCCUPATIONS: Businessman; justice of
ᵉ peace

ᴹOTHER: Elizabeth Speer Buchanan; b. Lancaster
ᵒunty, Pa., 1767; d. Greensburg, Pa., 1833

ᴮROTHERS: William Speer (1805–1826); George Wash-
ᵍton (1808–1832); Edward Young (1811–1895)

ᴵSTERS: Mary (1789–1791); Jane (1793–1839); Maria
ᵗ795–1849); Sarah (1798–1825); Elizabeth (1800–1801);
ᴴarriet (1802–1839)

ᴴOME: Wheatland, Lancaster, Pa.

ᴱDUCATION: Attended Old Stone Academy; graduated
ᵒm Dickinson College in 1809

ᴿELIGIOUS AFFILIATION: Presbyterian

ᴼCCUPATION BEFORE PRESIDENCY: Lawyer

ᴾRE-PRESIDENTIAL OFFICES: Member of Pa. Legis-
ᵗure; Member of U.S. House of Representatives; Minister
ᵗ Russia; Member of U.S. Senate; Secretary of State;
ᴹinister to Great Britain

ᴬGE AT INAUGURATION: 65

ᴼCCUPATION AFTER PRESIDENCY: Retired

ᴰEATH: Lancaster, Pa., June 1, 1868

ᴾLACE OF BURIAL: Woodward Hill Cemetery, Lan-
ᶜster, Pa.

ᴱLECTION OF 1856

CANDIDATES	ELECTORAL VOTE	POPULAR VOTE
James Buchanan Democratic	174	1,832,955
John C. Frémont Republican	114	1,339,932
Millard Fillmore American (Know-Nothing)	8	871,731

*Harriet Lane Johnston (above) was White House host-
ess for her uncle, James Buchanan. Her private collection of superb paintings became the nucleus of
the Smithsonian's National Collection of Fine Arts.*

THE BUCHANAN ADMINISTRATION

INAUGURATION: March 4, 1857; the Capitol, Washington, D.C.

VICE PRESIDENT: John C. Breckinridge

SECRETARY OF STATE: Lewis Cass; Jeremiah S. Black
(from Dec. 17, 1860)

SECRETARY OF THE TREASURY: Howell Cobb;
Philip F. Thomas (from Dec. 12, 1860); John A. Dix (from
Jan. 15, 1861)

SECRETARY OF WAR: John B. Floyd; Joseph Holt
(from Jan. 18, 1861)

ATTORNEY GENERAL: Jeremiah S. Black; Edwin M.
Stanton (from Dec. 22, 1860)

POSTMASTER GENERAL: Aaron V. Brown; Joseph
Holt (from March 14, 1859); Horatio King (from Feb. 12,
1861)

SECRETARY OF THE NAVY: Isaac Toucey

SECRETARY OF THE INTERIOR: Jacob Thompson

SUPREME COURT APPOINTMENT: Nathan Clifford

35th CONGRESS (March 4, 1857–March 4, 1859):
Senate: 36 Democrats; 20 Republicans; 8 Others
House: 118 Democrats; 92 Republicans; 26 Others

36th CONGRESS (March 4, 1859–March 4, 1861):
Senate: 36 Democrats; 26 Republicans; 4 Others
House: 114 Republicans; 92 Democrats; 31 Others

STATES ADMITTED: Minnesota (1858); Oregon (1859);
Kansas (1861)

ABRAHAM LINCOLN

Abraham Lincoln, said John Hay, was "the greatest character since Christ." And for millions of his countrymen, during his lifetime and now, the sixteenth President was, and remains, an American messiah, murdered on Good Friday, a martyr to assaulted truth. Yet despite his grandeur, he is revered as a homespun hero, as humble as a copper penny, a parent's last word on the virtues of honesty, thrift, and moral simplicity.

America's judgment of Lincoln has not, however, been uniform. He has been denounced for denying freedom to the South on the pretense of saving freedom for the Union. Wendell Phillips, the abolitionist, thought him "a first rate *second*-rate man." To Confederate journalists he was "the Ourang-Outang at the White House" and "the Abolition Emperor."

Even the admiring Hay could lament Lincoln's "unconscious assumption of superiority." William H. Herndon, his law partner and biographer, noted that his ambition was "a little engine that knew no rest" and remarked that anyone "who thinks Lincoln calmly gathered his robes about him, waiting for the people to call him, has a very erroneous knowledge of Lincoln. He was always calculating and planning ahead." Neither divine nor demoniac, always very human, Lincoln reveled in politics. He could dodge, evade, and connive when necessary. But he rose above politics into a timeless greatness that would ultimately suffer no partisan label. He became the embodiment of American idealism and, in historian David Donald's excellent phrase, "the collective wish-fulfillment of the American people."

"It is a great folly," Lincoln once told a biographer, "to attempt to make anything out of me or my early life. It can all be condensed into a single sentence; and that sentence you will find in Gray's *Elegy*: 'The short and simple

Abraham Lincoln, in an 1862 daguerreotype by Mathew Brady

annals of the poor.'" Lincoln was born on February 12, 1809, in a one-room, dirt-floored log cabin in backwoods Kentucky. Thomas Lincoln, his father, was a Baptist, a Jacksonian, and a carpenter by trade. Able only to scrawl his name, Thomas was no inspiration to young Abe, whose bookish aversion to frontier chores he grew to resent. Nancy Hanks Lincoln, his mother, was evidently an illegitimate child. Lincoln himself, according to Herndon, said candidly: "My mother was a bastard, was the daughter of a nobleman so called of Virginia." And to that unnamed Southern aristocrat Lincoln attributed any mental distinction he possessed. To the stoop-shouldered, religious Nancy he gave all his love. "I owe everything I am to her," he said.

In 1811, when Abe was two, the family moved about ten miles northeast to Knob Creek, Kentucky. Five years later, facing eviction, Thomas moved again, this time to Indiana. He erected his new home at Pigeon Creek; Abe, seven, helped to build it. When Lincoln was nine, his mother died. A year later Thomas married Sarah Bush Johnston, a widow. To the cabin in Indiana Sarah brought her own three children and much love. According to Lincoln's friend Ward Hill Lamon, she cared for Abe and his sister Sarah as if they were her own, feeding, washing, and clothing them, making them look, in her own words, "a little more human." She took a fast shine to Abe: "His mind and mine—what little I had—seemed to run together." She encouraged his reading and apparently convinced Thomas Lincoln to let the boy be.

The years in Indiana, Lincoln later recalled, were "pretty pinching times." The family ate adequately, but they worked hard for any comfort they had. And young Abe pitched in, plowing, tending the fire, planting seed, picking berries. He became prodigious with an axe: Dennis Hanks, his cousin, recalled that if "you heard him fellin' trees in a clearin', you would say that there was three men at work by the way the trees fell."

To help his father financially, Abe hired himself out as a handy man. Some employers,

When Sarah Lincoln (above) was told of her stepson's murder, she said, "I knowed they'd kill him."

such as John Romaine, were not pleased with him. "He worked for me," said Romaine, "but was always reading and thinking. I used to get mad at him for it. I say he was awful lazy. He would laugh and talk, crack jokes and tell stories all the time. . . . He said to me . . . that his father taught him to work but he never taught him to love it."

But for all his delight in people, talk, and sport, he was largely a loner: alone in the fields and forests of the frontier. "Silence," Carl Sandburg writes, "found him for her own. In the making of him, the element of silence was immense."

Lincoln possessed a quick and inquiring mind that cut to the marrow of facts and ideas and that saw their relationships with intuitive force. This mind must have been a birthright, for in Lincoln's words, in "unpolitical" Indiana "there was absolutely nothing to excite ambition for education." In the one-room schools of the day, formal education embraced nothing more than reading (*Dilworth's Speller*), a little writing, and, as Lincoln later said, "cipherin' to the rule of three."

Despite this stifling environment, Lincoln rose to knowledge. Wherever he could find or make light, he read: *Aesop's Fables, Robinson Crusoe*, the Bible. Even at work in the field, when his horse rested, Lincoln's book would be out of his pocket. Books like Parson Weems's lyrical life of Washington affected him deeply. When he borrowed the Weems book and got it wet, he worked three days on a farm to pay for it and own it.

For all his introspection, Lincoln was a powerful young man—tough, muscular, a rough foe in any bout. By nineteen, he was six feet four inches tall. Despite a relatively small chest and a slim waist, he had powerful shoulders and large limbs.

In February, 1830, Thomas Lincoln pulled up stakes again, this time moving to Macon County in Illinois. The next year, Abe struck out on his own: hired by Denton Offut, he worked on a flatboat carrying goods to New Orleans. It was a decisive trip, for Offut took a liking to him and offered him a job as a clerk in a general store and mill in New Salem, Illinois. And on this passage Lincoln first saw the horror of slavery: Negroes in chains, whipped and sold like cattle.

He arrived in New Salem in July, 1831, and soon thereafter squared off in a wrestling match with the town tough, Jack Armstrong. Some say he beat Armstrong; others call it a draw. But unmistakably, Lincoln won Jack's and the townspeople's respect. Affable behind the counter, good to children, obliging to widows (for whom he chopped wood), Lincoln earned a reputation for kindness, reliability, and honesty. Also, clerking afforded him leisure for reading. Weems gave way to Voltaire and Thomas Paine, to Burns and Blackstone, to Indiana statutes and the Constitution, to Shakespeare (*Macbeth* was his favorite). Friends lent him books, the cooper opened his shop to him at night so that he could read by a fire of shavings, and

schoolmaster Mentor Graham polished Lincoln's command of the English language.

In 1832 Lincoln served one brief term as a soldier in the field. When the Sauk, under Black Hawk, took to the warpath, the governor issued a call for volunteers, and Lincoln promptly signed up. He saw no battle, but served competently in two independent companies as a scout.

Returning to New Salem, the popular Lincoln campaigned for a seat in the Illinois general assembly as an anti-Jackson Whig. His approach was disarmingly to the point: "Fellow Citizens, I presume you all know who I am. I am humble Abraham Lincoln. . . . My politics are short and sweet like the old woman's dance. I am in favour of a national bank. I am in favour of the internal improvement system and a high protective tariff. . . . If elected, I shall be thankful; if not, it will be all the same." Predictably, Lincoln lost this first election in hard-nosed Jacksonian territory. But he won almost all the votes of his neighbors, Democrats or not.

He was soon back in the grocery business, in partnership with William F. Berry, who had served with him during the Black Hawk War. On credit and on Lincoln's high reputation in the town, the two veterans took over three stores. But the enterprises foundered: Berry liked liquor too much, and Lincoln, the law, which he was studying in spare moments. It took him fifteen years of self-denial to pay off all his—and Berry's—creditors.

When the job of postmaster fell vacant in May, 1833, Lincoln was named to the office. In charge of the mails, he could be less than efficient, keeping his postal receipts in an old blue sock and the mail in his hat. But on his rounds, he was more than dutiful. He would walk miles to deliver a letter he knew was eagerly awaited. The postmaster's salary was based on receipts and ranged from $25 to $80 a year. So, probably through the influence of a Democratic friend, Lincoln was offered the more lucrative post of deputy county surveyor. He learned about surveying by poring over books late into the night.

Meanwhile, love had found Lincoln, in the person of Ann Rutledge, daughter of a tavern keeper. Ann was auburn-haired, blue-eyed, slender, and fair. Lincoln loved her, courted her, and became engaged to her. But Ann died of typhoid, and Lincoln was thrust into a profound melancholy.

A seat in the Illinois assembly remained Lincoln's goal: when he sought election again in 1834, he won. Through the first session of the legislature, he remained observant and silent in his new sixty-dollar suit. But in succeeding sessions, he rose to the leadership of his party, becoming the Whigs' perennial candidate for speaker of the house in the strongly Democratic assembly. He supported the removal of the state capital to Springfield, to which he himself moved in 1837. In the capital, he boarded free with a tradesman named Joshua Speed, who took pity on his poverty and melancholy face. These legislative years saw a maturing of Lincoln's moderate Whig philosophy and his development as an adroit partisan advocate and orator. Admitted to the bar in 1836, he fared well, not only as a capital attorney, but also as a circuit lawyer.

Of primary interest in his Springfield years is his position on slavery. The Illinois constitution of 1818 had granted the vote to all adult white male residents, without qualification. Consequently, Lincoln's campaign appeal of 1836 that "all whites . . . who pay taxes or bear arms" be given the vote was radical only in his suggestion that taxpaying females be allowed to vote.

Indeed, Lincoln remained highly ambivalent on the subject of slavery. In response to the rise in Illinois of overt antislavery sentiment, the Illinois legislature in 1837 passed resolutions condemning abolitionism and denying the right of the federal government either to abridge slavery in the states or to abolish it without a vote in the District of Columbia. In a dissenting resolution, Lincoln and a friend, Dan Stone, addressed themselves not only to abolitionism, but to the institution of slavery itself. Slavery, they said, was "founded on both injustice and bad policy. . . ." On the other hand, they argued, the abolition of slavery was also wrong because "the promulgation of aboli-

tion doctrines tends rather to increase than to abate" the evils of slavery. As for the role of the federal government, Lincoln and Stone agreed that the federal government could not constitutionally interfere with slavery in any state but that it could abolish it in the District of Columbia, though "that power ought not to be exercised unless" the people of the District so requested.

But all was not politics in Springfield. Lincoln had fallen in love again. As a popular and respected legislator, he had access to the hub of Springfield's social life, the Ninian Edwards' mansion, which was overseen by Mrs. Elizabeth Todd Edwards, sister of Mary Todd of Lexington, Kentucky. Twenty-one-year-old Mary was well educated and charming, if high tempered. In its initial stage, her courtship with Lincoln lasted for about twelve months, and their wedding was set for January 1, 1841.

What happened at that first scheduled wedding of Mary and Abraham has been the subject of passionate controversy. Some biographers insist that Lincoln simply did not show up. Others say that he went to Mary and said he could not go through with the marriage. There is no disagreement, however, over the fact that after he left Mary Todd, Lincoln experienced a profound emotional breakdown lasting almost a year and a half. Joshua Speed and Speed's mother nursed him back to mental health.

By mid-1842, Lincoln was moving toward stability, and Mary Todd was still willing. They reconciled and repledged their troth. On November 4, 1842, they were married in an Episcopal ceremony. A week later, Lincoln concluded a business letter with an enigmatic remark: "Nothing new here except my marrying, which to me, is matter of profound wonder."

Lincoln's marriage to Mary was indisputably rocky. They fought hard and bitterly, often and audibly. Lincoln seems to have met Mary's assaults with a saddened forbearance, avoiding conflict when possible. A common love for their children bound them together: Robert, the eldest, who would go on to Exeter and Harvard and service as

Secretary of War under Presidents Garfield and Arthur; Edward, who would die at three; William, who would die at eleven in the White House; and frail Thomas ("Tad"), who was afflicted with a stammer.

In 1846 Lincoln was elected to the Thirtieth Congress by the largest majority in the history of his district. When he arrived in Washington, the United States was only several weeks short of victory in the Mexican War. In Congress Lincoln joined the shrill Whig attack on the Democratic President, James K. Polk. On January 12, 1848, Congressman Lincoln explained his position. He rejected as the "sheerest deception" Polk's claim that the first American blood spilled by Mexicans was spilled on American soil. Mexico was not the aggressor; the United States was. Back home in his Illinois district, the reaction to Lincoln's stand against the war was one of fury and shock. But the congressman stood his ground. "Allow the President to invade a neighboring nation whenever he shall deem it necessary to repel an invasion . . ." Lincoln wrote, "and you allow him to make war at pleasure. . . ."

In Congress Lincoln consistently favored the exclusion of slavery in the territories ceded by Mexico, but he still remained opposed to federal interference with slavery in the states where it already existed. A lame-duck congressman (by prearrangement with other party leaders in Illinois), he introduced, in January, 1849, an amendment to a resolution instructing the Committee on the District of Columbia to report out a bill abolishing slavery in the District. Lincoln urged that children born of slaves in Washington after January 1, 1850, should be free, but should be apprenticed to their masters until they came of age. Masters wishing to free a slave would be compensated by the federal government. All fugitive slaves escaping into the District, under Lincoln's plan, were to be returned to their masters. The resolution did not become law.

In 1848 Lincoln took to the stump for the Whig presidential candidate, Zachary Taylor. He organized demonstrations and rallies and toured New England in a bid to unite Whigs and Free-Soilers behind the war hero. Taylor won, and after the inauguration the congressman looked for a patronage plum: the office of commissioner of the general land office. When he failed to get this position, a disillusioned Lincoln, now aged forty,

Vandalia was the Illinois capital until 1839. When Lincoln joined the legislature in 1834, the brick State-house, although only ten years old, was in such disrepair that laws had to be framed amidst falling plaster.

retired for a five-year lull in public political activity. Again he was a circuit lawyer, a natural politician who liked a good joke.

But the "irrepressible conflict" was approaching, presaged even more formidably by the passage in 1854 of the Kansas-Nebraska Act. Sired by Illinois's Democratic senator, Stephen A. Douglas, the act, in effect, opened up the entire area of the Louisiana Purchase to slavery. In the Northwest the reaction to the act was bitter and violent. On March 20, 1854, anger gave way to organized political rebellion when a coalition of Whigs, Free-Soilers, and antislavery Democrats met at Ripon, Wisconsin, and formed the Republican party.

Lincoln joined the new party in 1856 and campaigned hard for its first presidential candidate, John C. Frémont. By plumping for the party slate, he built his own reputation, county by county. According to Horace White, secretary of the Illinois Republican state committee, Lincoln was "one of the shrewdest politicians of the state. . . ." Nobody, White said, "knew better than he what was passing in the minds of the people. Nobody knew better how to turn things to advantage politically, and nobody was readier to take such advantage, provided it did not involve dishonorable means."

Two days after the inauguration of President Buchanan in 1857, Chief Justice Roger B. Taney's heavily Southern Supreme Court handed down its decision in the Dred Scott case: it ruled that slaves were property, and declared the Missouri Compromise unconstitutional. In Springfield, Senator Douglas defended the Court's decision. "The Courts," Douglas said, "are tribunals prescribed by the Constitution. . . . Hence, whoever resists the final decision of the highest judicial tribunal aims a deadly blow at our whole Republican system of government. . . ."

Lincoln, now emerging as the major spokesman for free-soil Republicanism, spoke in Springfield on June 26, 1857. He derided Douglas' pious homily on the Court's pre-eminence, pointing out that Douglas himself had defied the Court's ruling on the United States Bank by applauding Presi-

dent Jackson's refusal to abide by its decision. Lincoln condemned the alliance of American business interests, educators, and theologians, who were, he said, joining forces to imprison the Negro forever. Any man who justifies the enslavement of others, he added, justifies his own. If color is the excuse, and the lighter man has a right to enslave the darker, the lighter may himself be enslaved by a still lighter man. If intellectual superiority justifies slavery, all men are at the mercy of those more brilliant than they. If business interest justifies slavery, anyone with an interest in a man, white or black, may enslave him.

Lincoln's logic, now fired by political passion, was unassailable. To Douglas' statement that Lincoln's views were held only by people who wanted "to vote, and eat, and sleep, and marry with Negroes," Lincoln replied that the fact that he did not want to have a Negro woman for a slave did not imply that he must have her for a wife. Could he not just leave her alone? "In some respects," he said, "she certainly is not my equal; but in her natural right to eat the bread she earns with her own hands without asking leave of any one else, she is my equal, and the equal of all others."

Lincoln's reply to Douglas initiated a verbal exchange that thrust him into national fame. On June 16, 1858, he was named by the Republicans to run for Douglas' Senate seat. That same day, he delivered his acceptance speech at the Illinois Republican state convention. Noting the rise of impassioned agitation against slavery, Lincoln told his party: "In *my* opinion, it *will* not cease, until a *crisis* shall have been reached, and passed." Then he turned to the language of the Bible: " 'A house divided against itself cannot stand.' I believe this government cannot endure, permanently half *slave* and half *free*. I do not expect the Union to be *dissolved*—I do not expect the house to *fall*—but I *do* expect it will cease to be divided. It will become *all* one thing, or *all* the other. Either the *opponents* of slavery, will arrest the further spread of it, and place it where the public mind shall rest in the belief that it is in course of ultimate extinction; or its *advocates* will push it forward, till it shall become alike in *all* the States, *old* as well as *new—North* as well as *South*."

To a critic who complained that the speech was too strong, Lincoln replied: "If I had to draw a pen across my record, and erase my whole life from sight, and I had one poor gift or choice as to what I should save from the wreck, I should choose that speech and leave it to the world unerased."

Then he challenged Douglas to a series of debates which began at Ottawa, Illinois, on August 21, 1858, and ended at Alton on October 15, amidst banners, brass bands, raucous crowds, and sweating reporters. At Freeport, on August 27, Douglas made a major ideological concession—his famed "Freeport Doctrine"—that would cost him Southern Democratic support and would nourish Democratic disunion. To Lincoln's question, "Can the people of a United States territory, in any lawful way, against the wish of any citizen of the United States, exclude slavery from its limits prior to the formation of a state constitution?" Douglas answered Yes. Further, he said, "it matters not what way the Supreme Court may hereafter decide as to . . . whether slavery may or may not go into a territory under the Constitution, the people have the lawful means to introduce it or exclude it as they please. . . ."

At the last debate, at Alton, Douglas assailed Lincoln's "house divided" speech as a "slander upon the immortal framers of our Constitution," who founded the country, he said, both free and slave, under state sovereignties. He ridiculed Lincoln's egalitarian view of the Declaration of Independence, which was meant, Douglas said, for colonial and British whites only. And he condemned Lincoln's "crusade against the Supreme Court" following the Dred Scott decision.

Lincoln replied that if the Founding Fathers were as wise as Douglas agreed, why did he defy their permissive attitude on slavery by introducing his divisive Kansas-Nebraska bill? Lincoln envisioned new United States territories open to "*free white people everywhere*—the world over. . . ." He dismissed

Attended by a Negro, Lincoln and Douglas engage in "The Undecided Political Prize Fight" of 1860.

Douglas' charges that he sought a sectional war over slavery or favored "introducing a perfect social and political equality between the white and black races. . . ." The whole question, Lincoln said, was reduced to a choice between "the common right of humanity" or "the divine right of kings."

Actually, the debaters were less at odds than they appeared to be. Lincoln fully shared Douglas' horror of miscegenation. "Agreed for once—a thousand times agreed," he said in 1857. "There are white men enough to marry all the white women, and black men enough to marry all the black women; and so let them be married." Though affirming in July, 1858, that he had "always hated slavery . . . as much as any Abolitionist," he insisted that he had never intended to do anything about it where it already existed. And finally he declared in Chicago on July 10, 1858, that he wished that all talk of "inferior" people be discarded. Yet only two months later, in Charleston, Illinois, he contradicted himself:

"I will say then that I am not, nor ever have been in favor of bringing about in any way the social and political equality of the white and black races—that I am not nor ever have been in favor of making voters or jurors of negroes, nor of qualifying them to hold office, nor to intermarry with white people. . . . And inasmuch as they cannot so live, while they do remain together there must be the position of superior and inferior, and I as much as any other man am in favor of having the superior position assigned to the white race."

In the Senate election, held on November 2, 1858, Lincoln polled a popular majority of some four thousand votes over his opponent. But Douglas, through gerrymandered apportionment, won electoral control of the assembly, which re-elected him to the Senate 54 to 46. Lincoln described his reaction to the defeat in words that would one day be echoed by another Illinoisan, Adlai E. Stevenson II. Likening himself to the little boy who stubbed his toe, he said, "It hurt too bad to laugh, and he was too big to cry." But friends assured a disappointed Lincoln that more and more influential people were eying him for the Presidency. Replied Lincoln, "I . . . admit that I am ambitious, and would like to be President . . . but there is no such good luck in store for me. . . ."

Still, friends pressed the issue, urging Lincoln to make himself even better known. Calls for speeches poured in from Iowa, Pennsylvania, Missouri, New York. On February 27, 1860, at Cooper Institute in Manhattan, he argued wholly from tradition, citing the personal attitudes and constitutional provisions of the Founding Fathers to support a policy of nonintervention with slavery in states where it existed and the barring of it in the territories. Lincoln denied that the Republican appeal for the restriction of slavery was sectional, urging the South to give it a chance at the polls. George Washington himself, he said, had heartily signed Congress' Northwest Ordinance barring the extension of slavery. Was Washington sectional, too?

Rejecting the extremism of both abolitionists and secessionists, Lincoln disproved Taney's claim that the Constitution "distinctly and expressly" affirmed the right of property in a slave. The Constitution, he said, certainly guaranteed property. But as for

The country saw a determined Abraham Lincoln in this medal from the 1860 presidential campaign.

the slave, Lincoln explained, the Constitution cited him specifically as a "person," alluding to his master's claim over him solely in terms of "service or labor which may be due." To the South's claim that the election of a Republican President would destroy the Union, Lincoln replied: "That is cool. A highwayman holds a pistol to my ear, and mutters through his teeth, 'Stand and deliver, or I shall kill you, and then you will be a murderer!'" Slaveowners, he said, would apparently be appeased only if opponents of slavery would agree that slavery was morally proper and should be given "a full national recognition . . . as a legal right, and a social blessing." The South, he said, was demanding that the righteous, not the unrighteous, be called to repentance. "*Right,*" Lincoln concluded, "*makes might. . . .*" New York applauded.

Lincoln moved on to Providence, then to New Hampshire, where he was hailed by Governor Frederick Smith as "the next President of the United States." In May his political ship made for home port at the Illinois Republican state convention in Decatur. When John Hanks, Lincoln's old Mississippi flatboat companion, entered the convention hall bearing two rails allegedly split by Abe, the delegates erupted with joy.

The Republican National Convention of 1860, held in Chicago, ratified the decision made at Decatur. Senator William H. Seward of New York, who had called American civil war "irrepressible," entered the convention city a brassy and confident candidate. Others in the field were Salmon P. Chase, Edward Bates, and Simon Cameron.

A great roar went up for Seward when he was nominated, but there was an even greater cry for Lincoln. "The uproar" for Abe, a journalist reported, "was beyond description. Imagine all the hogs ever slaughtered in Cincinnati giving their death squeals together. . . ." Then the Republican party voted. Needed to win: 233 votes. First ballot: Seward, 173½; Lincoln, 102 votes. Favorite-son votes for Bates, Cameron, Chase, and others. Second ballot: Seward, 184½; Lincoln, 181. "I've got him," cried Lincoln in Springfield when the news flashed to the capital. Third ballot: Lincoln, 231½. Ohio rose: four votes for Lincoln, Republican candidate for President of the United States.

In Springfield a nervous Lincoln, who had played ball during the day to relieve his tension, heard the news and went off to tell Mary. He seemed calm, Lamon said, "but a close observer could detect in his countenance the indications of deep emotion."

The Republican platform of 1860 called for noninterference in slave states and for exclusion of slavery from the territories. It pledged a homestead act to grant free land to settlers. In addition, the party called for a rigid tariff to protect burgeoning American industries, railroad subsidies to unite the country economically, improved mail and telegraph lines, and whatever would aid the development of a brash, progressive American capitalism.

At the Democratic convention, meeting at Charleston, South Carolina, eight cotton states, indignant over the party's refusal to endorse slavery, withdrew from the hall. Rump conventions nominated Douglas as the official Democratic candidate; John C. Breckinridge of Kentucky as the Southern candidate; and Tennessee's John Bell as candidate of the new and moderate National Constitution Union party. Lincoln directed a campaign strategy aimed at further deepening the critical schisms within the Democratic party. His running mate, Senator Hannibal Hamlin of Maine, was an ex-Democrat who had turned Republican.

It was not an inspiring campaign. Northern propagandists portrayed the politically sophisticated Lincoln as an ingenuous but patriotic plowman sacrificing farm and security to save his country; or, despite Lincoln's oft-stated compromises on slavery, as a veritable abolitionist. Nor was the South lacking its own barrel of distortions. A Republican victory, it declared, would mean the end of states' rights, of respect for private property, and of freedom itself.

Though his three opponents polled 60 per cent of the popular vote in the election of November 6, 1860, Lincoln won 180 electoral votes out of 303, carrying all eighteen free states. But Republican joy was overshadowed by dark clouds of rebellion in the South, now thoroughly persuaded that Lincoln meant to destroy its economy and political foundations.

In Congress compromise measures were advanced, among them the Crittenden proposal to sustain existing slavery and to divide the territories between slavery and freedom at the old Missouri Compromise line. But while the President-elect maintained public silence, he moved powerfully behind the scenes, instructing Republicans to vote against any compromise measure that allowed the extension of slavery.

The Southern storm broke on December 20, 1860, in a slow roll of secessionist thunder. On that day, South Carolina declared at Charleston that "the union now subsisting between South Carolina and other States under the name of the United States of America is hereby dissolved." On February 4, 1861, seven Southern states met at Montgomery to proclaim the Confederate States of America. The threat of decades had become a reality: the house was divided.

On February 11, Lincoln bade farewell to Springfield: "To this place, and the kindness of these people," he said, "I owe everything. . . . I now leave, not knowing when, or whether ever, I may return, with a task before me greater than that which rested upon Washington."

Lincoln's journey to the national capital was protracted to twelve days to permit speeches and receptions along the way. In Philadelphia, word reached the party of a plot to murder Lincoln in Baltimore, and plans were made to curtail the President-elect's journey immediately and to send him by private coach to Washington. While agreeing to bypass Baltimore, Lincoln insisted on going ahead with Washington's Birthday ceremonies at Independence Hall, which were highlighted by his raising of a 34-star flag, hailing Kansas' admission to the Union as a free state.

Within hours, Lincoln was hidden as an invalid in a Pullman berth, and he began his secret midnight journey to Washington. At six o'clock in the morning, Saturday, February 23, 1861, a muffler around his neck, he slipped into the Capital and quietly checked in at the Willard Hotel. There he received well-wishers, heard patronage requests, and organized his Cabinet. Delegates to the celebrated "Peace Conference"—an attempt by representatives from twenty-one states to restore the Union—met with him, but Lincoln was firm before all insistence that in the interest of national unity he permit the extension of slavery: "My course," he said, "is as plain as a turnpike road. It is marked out by the Constitution."

On March 4, 1861, seated in an open carriage with Buchanan, protected at all points of the route to the Capitol by cavalry and infantry and by riflemen perched in windows, Lincoln rode to his destiny. Speaking from the east portico of the Capitol, he offered massive reassurances and concessions to the South: "I have no purpose, directly

THE EAGLE'S NEST.

Chillingly ferocious, the Union eagle crushes its deformed and rebellious offspring in this 1861 cartoon.

412

or indirectly, to interfere with the institution of slavery in the States where it exists." He cited the Republicans' platform promise to maintain states' rights. He abjured an armed invasion of states by any domestic power as "the gravest of crimes" and upheld the Fugitive Slave Law's provision that runaway slaves must be returned to their masters. Then Lincoln turned to the crisis of secession. Even if the Constitution were merely a voluntary contract, he reasoned, one party to that contract could not declare it null and void. The Union was inviolable.

"I therefore consider that . . . the Union is unbroken," Lincoln declared, "and . . . I shall take care, as the Constitution itself expressly enjoins upon me, that the laws of the Union be faithfully executed in all the States." In pursuit of this policy, he added, "there needs to be no bloodshed or violence; and there shall be none, unless it be forced upon the national authority." Then the President called the South back home: "In *your* hands, my dissatisfied fellow countrymen, and not in *mine*, is the momentous issue of civil war. The government will not assail *you*. You can have no conflict, without being yourselves the aggressors. . . ."

Then Chief Justice Taney arose. The author of the Dred Scott decision, his hands shaking, his face ashen, stepped forward to administer the oath of office: "I, Abraham Lincoln, do solemnly swear that I will faithfully execute the Office of President of the United States, and will to the best of my Ability, preserve, protect and defend the Constitution of the United States." He was President.

But the South had made its decision; there was no going back. By the time Lincoln took his oath, Confederates had seized all federal forts and Navy yards in the states under their control, except Fort Pickens in Pensacola, Florida, and Fort Sumter at Charleston, South Carolina.

Lincoln's Cabinet was a formidable collection of Whigs, converted Democrats, and moderate and radical Republicans. His primary appointments were all men of extraordinary ability and integrity: William H.

The indulgent Lincoln ignored his son Tad's mischief. "Let him run," he remarked. "There's time enough for him to learn his letters and get pokey."

Seward, the antislavery senator from New York, as Secretary of State; the abolitionist Republican Salmon P. Chase of Ohio as Secretary of the Treasury; Simon Cameron of Pennsylvania as Secretary of War (he was replaced in January, 1862, by the articulate, unreconstructed but efficient Democrat Edwin M. Stanton); and Gideon Welles of Connecticut in the critical post of Secretary of the Navy. It was a Cabinet with massive potential for inner dispute, but it functioned well, largely through Lincoln's own personal ability to separate chaff from wheat.

Early in the administration, however, Lincoln's authority was challenged by Secretary Seward. The New Yorker clearly considered Lincoln his inferior in education, political experience, and good judgment, and he moved swiftly to establish his position as *de facto* President. In an incredible memorandum to Lincoln on April 1, 1861, Seward lamented what he called the President's lack of firm policies, domestic or foreign, after one month in office. He urged Lincoln, among other things, to shift his emphasis from slavery to Unionism and to divert attention from American disunion by precipitating a war with Spain and France. Further, he said, if the President was unwilling to pursue these policies, he would do it himself. To this contemptuous and irresponsible letter, President Lincoln responded with quiet grandeur. Whatever had to be done by executive authority, he told Seward, he would do as President. "Still . . . I wish, and suppose I am entitled to have, the advice of all the cabinet."

War now seemed imminent as the South demanded the evacuation of Fort Sumter. On the day after his inauguration, Lincoln had received word from the fort's commander that he and his men had scant provisions in the face of still silent Confederate shore batteries. A month later, the President had still not decided whether to provision the fort or to arm it further to repel a threatened Confederate assault. Ultimately, he decided to send food to the fort, making clear his decision against sending arms.

At 4:30 A.M. on April 12, 1861, the Confederate States of America fired upon Sumter. They were the first shots in a war that would kill 600,000 American men. Lincoln moved quickly to meet the assault. He called for 75,000 volunteers and ordered a blockade of the South. The Capital city itself made new preparations for siege. Virginia, angered by what it considered Lincoln's despotic call for volunteers, left the Union, followed by Arkansas, North Carolina, and Tennessee.

On July 4, President Lincoln addressed a saddened special session of Congress. The Confederates, he said, knew full well that he had sent bread and not bullets to Sumter and that the fort, hemmed in by Confederate guns, could scarcely have attacked them. Why, then, the assault? To destroy, Lincoln said, "the visible authority of the Federal Union, and thus force it to immediate dissolution. . . . This issue," said the President, "embraces more than the fate of these United States. It presents to the whole family of man, the question, whether a constitutional republic, or a democracy . . . can, or cannot maintain its territorial integrity against its own domestic foes . . ."; whether, in fact, republics had an "inherent and fatal" flaw.

The United States, Lincoln declared, had no alternative: it must "resist force, employed for its destruction, by force, for its preservation."

On July 21, the North was decisively defeated at Bull Run (Manassas) in the first major encounter of the war. Lincoln replaced his field commander, General Irvin McDowell, with General George B. McClellan; he was confident that McClellan would press the war forward with dispatch. When, on November 1, General Winfield Scott, ill and cantankerous, resigned his post as general in chief of the Union forces over policy differences, McClellan was named his successor. But although he was an efficient organizer, McClellan proved to be dilatory in executing his plans and was smitten, besides, with an overweening egotism. He and Lincoln disagreed as to strategy; the President preferred a massive frontal assault at Manassas, while McClellan proposed a direct march from the rear on the Confederate capital at Richmond. In January, 1862, McClellan had still not begun his offensive, and an impatient Lincoln ordered him to move by February 22.

In early February, however, Lincoln deferred to McClellan's plan to march on Richmond. On March 8, the President reorganized the Army in four corps, relieving McClellan of all duties except those of commander of the Army of the Potomac. McClellan moved by water to the mouth of the James River, then up the Virginia peninsula between the James and the York rivers. In a series of bloody encounters he faced General Robert E. Lee, whose forces drove McClellan's men from the peninsula in the Seven Days' Battles, ending at Malvern Hill on July 1. When McClellan blamed Lincoln for not sending reinforcements, the President replied that he had sent as many as he could. Losses in the campaign were heavy, and Lincoln appealed for 300,000 more men.

The year 1862 was a bitter one for the President. In February his son, eleven-year-old Willie, died after a bout of cold and fever. Lincoln was shattered. Mary, who wore mourning black for almost two years, collapsed in "paroxysms of grief." Even the sorrowing President, immured in his own anguish, warned her on one occasion that she would have to be committed to a mental hospital if she could not control herself.

Stricken with family grief, and with the hard news of mounting Union casualties in a war he had hoped would be brief, Lincoln was also harassed by a divided and personally ambitious Cabinet; by abolitionists calling for total war on slavery and for the unconditional surrender of an occupied South; by the defeatism of those who demanded peace before Union; by uncooperative states; by the insubordinate and vacillating McClellan; by desertion in the Army; and by virulent abuse in the press.

"As a general rule," the President would say in his last public address, "I abstain from reading the reports of attacks upon myself, wishing not to be provoked by that to which I cannot properly offer an answer." But some attacks could not go unanswered. Among these was an assault by Horace Greeley, editor of the New York *Tribune*, in August, 1862. In an open letter to the President, Greeley berated Lincoln for capitulating to the South by failing to issue immediately a decree emancipating the slaves.

It is true that Lincoln vacillated on the slavery question. A political realist, he knew that basic institutions were not changed by the stroke of a pen or a sword or by the dictates of personal idealism; he realized that even when the North won the war it would still have to face the issues of slavery and lingering disloyalty. He could not go forward, he believed, unless the people were with him, step by step.

He had, however, appealed to the border states to free slaves gradually and to compensate their owners with the assistance of the federal government. Congress had already passed legislation freeing the slaves of "disloyal" masters and those in the District of Columbia and in the territories. Then, in July, 1862, the President summoned his Cabinet and laid before it for discussion an emancipation proclamation. Seward agreed on principle, but advised postponement. Current Union military reverses, he argued, might encourage some to consider the measure "the last *shriek* on our retreat." Lincoln concurred.

A month later, in his reply to Greeley, Lincoln placed the Union above all other considerations. "My paramount object in this struggle *is* to save the Union, and is *not*

The Monitor *(foreground) and the* Merrimac *exchange fire off Hampton Roads on March 9, 1862. The Merrimac finally retired, but neither vessel was seriously damaged in this first battle between ironclad warships.*

either to save or to destroy slavery. . . . What I do about slavery, and the colored race, I do because I believe it helps to save the Union; and what I forbear, I forbear because I do *not* believe it would help to save the Union. . . . I have here stated my purpose according to my view of *official* duty; and I intend no modification of my oft-expressed *personal* wish that all men everywhere could be free."

To restore the Union, Lincoln considered no measure ultimately too severe. "These rebels," he reasoned, "are violating the Constitution to destroy the Union; I will violate the Constitution, if necessary, to save the Union. . . ." Accordingly, President Lincoln unilaterally increased the size of the Army and Navy, imposed a blockade of the South, suspended the writ of habeas corpus where necessary, placed treason suspects in military custody, and forbade the use of the mails for "treasonable correspondence." In the actual military conduct of the war, Lincoln functioned literally as Commander in Chief, personally mapping strategy.

Despite such victories as the capture of Fort Donelson on the Cumberland River in Tennessee by General Ulysses S. Grant and the occupation of New Orleans by Flag Officer David Farragut, the North was being bled in battle after battle. Thirteen thousand Union troops became casualties at Shiloh in April. In August the Union suffered another crushing defeat at Bull Run. In September Stonewall Jackson captured twelve thousand Union troops at Harpers Ferry. Then Lee and Jackson met McClellan at Antietam on September 17, 1862, in a bloody but indecisive battle.

Now, on September 22, Lincoln issued the Preliminary Emancipation Proclamation, publishing the final version on January 1, 1863. "Things had gone from bad to worse," he confessed later, "until I felt we had reached the end of our rope on the plan of operations we had been pursuing; that we had about played our last card, and must change our tactics or lose the game."

The proclamation was issued, Lincoln said, as "an act of justice" as well as "a fit and necessary war measure." It freed slaves only in those areas of the Confederacy still in rebellion, not in Southern areas already occupied by the Union army, or in loyal slave states.

Secretary Seward was astonished: "We show our sympathy with slavery," he said, "by emancipating the slaves where we cannot reach them and holding them in bondage where we can set them free." And in fact the proclamation did not go nearly so far as the second Confiscation Act, which had provided freedom to slaves of disloyal owners, regardless of state of residence.

Documents notwithstanding, the war went on. An angry Lincoln fired McClellan on November 7, appointing General Ambrose Burnside to succeed him as commander of the Army of the Potomac. In January, 1863, after Lee's victory at Fredericksburg, Burnside was replaced by General Joseph Hooker, who would himself be succeeded by General George Meade in June.

In May, 1863, Chancellorsville saw a crushing defeat of the Union forces. Then, as Grant was laying siege to Vicksburg in Mississippi, Lee led the entire Army of Northern Virginia through the Shenandoah Valley to southern Pennsylvania, where he met the Union army in the greatest and most decisive battle of the war, at Gettysburg. After three days of battle (July 1–3) with massive losses on both sides, Lee was forced to withdraw on July 4 to a position west of Sharpsburg, where the flooded Potomac blocked his passage to Virginia. Lincoln issued orders to pursue the foe and to destroy his army. But Meade hesitated; the Potomac subsided, and Lee escaped. Lincoln despaired, blaming Meade: "He was within your grasp, and to have closed upon him would . . . have ended the war. As it is the war will be prolonged indefinitely."

Over five thousand men, in both gray and blue, had been killed in the savage encounter at Gettysburg; their bodies had littered the field. On November 19, 1863, President Lincoln joined in the consecration of a new national cemetery at the site where the men had fallen. Edward Everett, a renowned orator, held forth for two hours in a verbal crescendo filled with classical allusions. Then Lincoln rose to offer ten sentences of splendid simplicity that told—and still tell—what the war was all about:

"Four score and seven years ago our fathers brought forth on this continent, a new nation, conceived in Liberty, and dedicated to the proposition that all men are created equal.

"Now we are engaged in a great civil war, testing whether that nation, or any nation so conceived and so dedicated, can long endure. We are met on a great battle-field of that war. We have come to dedicate a portion of that field, as a final resting place for those who gave their lives that that nation might live. It is altogether fitting and proper that we should do this.

"But, in a larger sense, we can not dedicate—we can not consecrate—we can not hallow—this ground. The brave men, living and dead, who struggled here, have consecrated it, far above our poor power to add or detract. The world will little note, nor long remember what we say here, but it can never forget what they did here. It is for us the living, rather, to be dedicated here to the unfinished work which they who fought here have thus far so nobly advanced. It is rather for us to be here dedicated to the great task remaining before us—that from these honored dead we take increased devotion to that cause for which they gave the last full measure of devotion—that we here highly resolve that these dead shall not have died in vain—that this nation, under God, shall have a new birth of freedom—and that government of the people, by the people, for the people, shall not perish from the earth."

Response to this timeless address was largely disdainful. The Chicago *Times* asserted that the "cheek of every American must tingle with shame as he reads the silly, flat, and dish-watery utterances of the man who has to be pointed out to intelligent foreigners as the President of the United States." History, however, would agree with the Chicago *Tribune* that Abraham Lincoln's words would "live among the annals of men."

GEORGE B. McCLELLAN

Presidential candidate George McClellan had no more success *against* Lincoln in 1864 than General in Chief George McClellan had had *for* Lincoln in the Civil War's early days. A graduate of West Point (he ranked second in his class) and a veteran of the Mexican War, he had seemed the logical choice to lead the Union forces in 1861, but his egotism and overcautiousness plagued Lincoln. Calling his critics "traitors," McClellan continually asked for reinforcements and maintained that he could "do it all" if only he had more men. Lee and Jackson exploited his hesitancy during the bloody Peninsular Campaign. A Confederate general, speaking of the battle of Antietam, said that "Lee's army and everything it had" could have been captured by McClellan if he had not failed to pursue the retreating enemy. Shortly thereafter, an exasperated Lincoln sacked the man for whom the huge Army of the Potomac had been merely a "bodyguard." Two years later, the Democrats nominated McClellan for the Presidency, depicting him as a victim of administration callousness and an example of its ineptness. His chances were good until a series of Union victories re-established the voters' faith in Lincoln, who was returned to office. General McClellan soon faded from view but emerged to serve as governor of New Jersey from 1878 to 1881. The Connecticut-born general died at fifty-seven in 1885.

In late November, the Union cause was buttressed by Grant's victory at Chattanooga, where Confederate soldiers were driven from Tennessee. Grant's services to the Union were rewarded on March 12, 1864, when the ruddy field soldier was named, at last, general in chief of the Union armies.

In May, at the Wilderness (the area south of the Rapidan River near Richmond, Virginia), at Spotsylvania, and at Cold Harbor, Grant's forces suffered over sixty thousand casualties. Then Grant shifted his troops, moving south toward Petersburg, hoping to cut Richmond off from the Rebel states. Lee met him, and the siege of Petersburg began. For ten months Grant's forces were holed up in their trenches by a rugged Confederate defense.

On June 8 the Republican party nominated Lincoln at Baltimore for a second term. Andrew Johnson, a pro-Union Democrat who had been appointed military governor of Tennessee, was named for the Vice Presidency. A week earlier, Republican Radicals had met in Cleveland to nominate John C. Frémont for President. In August the Democrats chose General George B. McClellan to oppose Lincoln. Both the regular and rump Republican conventions affirmed support for a constitutional amendment to abolish all slavery forever, and Lincoln gave the proposed amendment his approval: "In the joint names of liberty and union," he said, "let us labor to give it legal form, and practical effect." (The President was to give the Thirteenth Amendment vital support in its consideration and adoption by Congress. Passed by the Senate in April, 1864, it was finally approved by the House of Representatives in January, 1865.)

It was a divisive political campaign. Lincoln was assailed in newspapers and campaign tracts. Horace Greeley pronounced the President "already beaten." Lincoln himself was doubtful about his chances of winning. "It seems exceedingly probable,"

Frank Bellew's drawing for Harper's Weekly *late in November of 1864 summed up the electorate's feeling: it was titled "Long Abraham a Little Longer."*

Harper's Weekly

he wrote confidentially, "that this Administration will not be re-elected."

But good news from the front—especially of the capture of Atlanta on September 1 by General William Sherman—aided Lincoln's cause. On September 22, Frémont withdrew. Even so, while Lincoln won the election on November 8 by an electoral victory of 212 to 21, his popular margin was not large: 2.2 million to 1.8 million.

On March 4, 1865, the President, appearing markedly older, again took the oath of office. He could look with satisfaction on the success of the Union armies. At Nashville, Union forces had decimated John B. Hood's troops. Sherman had completed his march to the sea, had forced the evacuation of Savannah, and had then swung north to seize Columbia, South Carolina. In February Union forces had occupied Charleston.

"Fondly do we hope—fervently do we pray—that this mighty scourge of war may speedily pass away," Lincoln said in his second Inaugural Address. "With malice toward none, with charity for all; with firmness in the right, as God gives us to see the right, let us strive on to finish the work we are in; to bind up the nation's wounds; to care for him who shall have borne the battle, and for his widow, and his orphan—to do all which may achieve and cherish a just, and a lasting, peace, among ourselves, and with all nations."

On April 3, the time for making peace was upon the President: Richmond had fallen. At 4 P.M., April 9, 1865, General Lee, given generous terms by Lincoln through Grant, surrendered at Appomattox Court House.

Lincoln's plans for Reconstruction were already well defined. In July, 1864, he had pocket vetoed Congress' vindictive Wade-Davis bill, which would have allowed the readmission of a state only after the majority of its electorate pledged past as well as present loyalty. At a preliminary conference with Confederate officials on board a ship off Hampton Roads, Virginia, on February 3, 1865, he had been conciliatory, excluding any punitive unconditional surrender by the South, promising pardons, urging only that

Southern Americans once again embrace the Constitution. He even suggested that the South might adopt the Thirteenth Amendment slowly, perhaps over a five-year period, and hinted at millions of dollars in federal compensation for freed slaves. And in a face-saving gesture to the South, he prevailed in his view that new state governments might be formed once 10 per cent of a state's qualified voters took an oath of loyalty to the United States and agreed to the emancipation of the slaves.

On April 11, 1865, Lincoln spoke from a White House window to a delirious victory throng. He called for an end to debate over the "pernicious abstraction" as to whether the Southern states had ever truly left the Union. "Finding themselves safely at home," Lincoln said, "it would be utterly immaterial whether they had ever been abroad."

The President cited Louisiana as a model of Reconstruction. He conceded that a larger electorate would be desirable and that "very

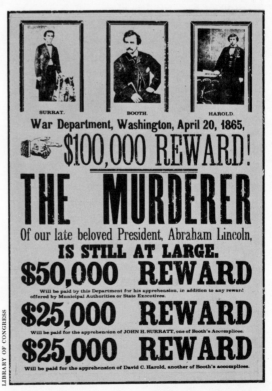

Twenty-eight men were directly involved in Booth's death; their bounties were finally awarded in 1866.

intelligent" Negroes might properly be given the vote. But which was the wiser course, he asked: to take Louisiana as it was and improve it, or to discard its antislavery government and start again? Louisiana, he said, was well on its way to harmony with the Union, now that it had empowered its legislators to give the Negro the vote, adopted a free constitution, and voted to ratify the Thirteenth Amendment. "We shall sooner have the fowl by hatching the egg than by smashing it," he said. Reconstruction, he warned, was a complex process to be pursued with realism and patience.

At 11 A.M., Good Friday, April 14, 1865, Lincoln met with his Cabinet, mapping Reconstruction until 2 P.M. Then the President went for a carriage drive with his wife. They rejoiced that the bitter war years were over and looked forward to that evening at the theater. General and Mrs. Grant were unable to join them in the presidential box at Ford's Theater, but Miss Clara Harris and Major Henry Rathbone—the daughter and stepson of Senator Ira Harris of New York —had accepted the Lincolns' invitation to see the comedy *Our American Cousin.*

The presidential party arrived late at Ford's. The actors stopped when they saw the President, and the band burst into "Hail to the Chief." Lincoln sat back, his hand in Mary's.

In a barroom near Ford's, a few minutes before 10 P.M., a twenty-six-year-old proslavery extremist, actor John Wilkes Booth, finished his drink; he departed and entered the theater. His movements planned step by step, Booth made his way to the door of the hallway leading to the President's box. Once inside, he bolted the door.

With a pistol in one hand and a dagger in the other, Booth opened the unguarded door of the box, aimed his pistol at Lincoln's head, and fired. Rathbone lunged at Booth, who stabbed him violently in the arm. Then the actor leaped from the box to the stage. Flashing his knife, Booth cried, "*Sic semper tyrannis!*" and escaped.

Lincoln sat mute and immobile, his head fallen forward. He was, said a doctor, fatally wounded. Booth's bullet had torn through the President's brain and had lodged behind an eye. Carried across the street to a boardinghouse owned by a Mr. Peterson, Lincoln was laid diagonally across a bed too small for his massive frame.

As the President lay dying, word spread that most of the Cabinet had been murdered, too. In fact, Seward, confined to bed by a bad fall, had been savagely bloodied by a Booth accomplice. But the rest of the Cabinet was safe.

At the Peterson house, Mrs. Lincoln, convulsed by a new, insupportable grief, moved closer to mental derangement. Robert, his head on the shoulder of Senator Sumner, sobbed aloud as his father slowly slipped away. At about six o'clock in the morning, April 15, 1865, rain began falling. At 7:22 A.M., Abraham Lincoln died.

His body lay in state in the East Room of the White House on a black-draped catafalque. Thousands of the nation's stunned citizens came to see the dead President. Some had seen him before, others had merely heard of him: "Old Abe," "Honest Abe," the "Rail Splitter" of Illinois and Indiana, the savior of the Union, dressed now in his First Inaugural suit for a final ascent to greatness.

On April 19, Lincoln's body was borne from the White House to begin a long journey to Illinois. The cortege stopped for homage in many cities along the way. Finally, on May 4, the coffin of the "Great Emancipator" was closed, and Lincoln was buried at Oak Ridge Cemetery in Springfield.

"What is to be will be," Lincoln had said, "or rather, I have found all my life as Hamlet says: 'There is a divinity that shapes our ends, Rough-hew them how we will.' " Healing when others wounded, hoping when others despaired, assuring when others feared, he grew in the Presidency taller than himself. He remains a symbol of liberty, his memory nourished by his own great words and deeds.

"Now," said a sorrowing Stanton for the nation, "he belongs to the ages."

—WILSON SULLIVAN

Abraham Lincoln

A PICTURE PORTFOLIO

*The Lincoln lantern above was attached to the end of a pole
and was carried in 1864 campaign parades in New York.*

The daguerreotype at right, made in 1846, is the earliest known photograph of Abraham Lincoln—freshman congressman from Illinois. Below is an 1868 view of part of Springfield's business section; Lincoln practiced law with the volatile William Herndon in the second building from the right. The men worked well as a professional team, but Herndon did not get on with Mrs. Lincoln and was much aggravated by Lincoln's reading newspapers aloud and permitting his children to use the office as a rumpus room. When Lincoln moved there, raw and sprawling Springfield was trying to comport itself properly as the new state capital, but hogs roamed at will in the streets, which often were seas of mud and impossible to navigate.

ON THE RISE

In 1834 Abraham Lincoln, still politically wet behind the ears, was elected to the legislature of the equally raw young state of Illinois. At the primitive capital, Vandalia, legislators wrangled and bargained, and Lincoln soon learned the techniques of political infighting. Sagacious vote swapping enabled him to lead the movement to transfer the capital to Springfield, his own base from 1837. Highly respected there, Lincoln still retained some rough edges. Once he leaped out of a window, trying to prevent a quorum because a vote would have hurt the state bank, one of his pet projects. But prudence began to temper him: when his biting satire provoked a challenge from an opponent, Lincoln shrewdly chose long cavalry broadswords as weapons, and his shorter-armed foe let matters drop. Lincoln also ran a thriving, if cluttered, law office (he kept an envelope marked, "When you can't find *it* any where else, look into this"). He and Mary lived modestly, but in a far more comfortable fashion than he had known as a youth in Kentucky and Indiana. A four-term legislator, the Lincoln of the early 1840's could no longer call himself "a piece of floating driftwood." Indeed, he was eagerly seeking a seat in the United States Congress and was thinking of even greater things.

ABRAHAM LINCOLN'S RESIDENCE.

At the end of 1843 the Lincolns moved into the frame house above, just beyond the Springfield business section. The house, lot, carriage shed, and barn—where Lincoln kept a horse and a milking cow—cost fifteen hundred dollars. Robert Todd Lincoln was five months old; three other sons would be born there, but only he would live to maturity. The family lived there until shortly after the November evening in 1860 when Lincoln returned from the telegraph office and announced, "Mary, we're elected." He was never again to return to Springfield.

THE "LITTLE GIANT"

If each State will only agree to mind its own business," boomed Stephen A. Douglas at Quincy, Illinois, in October, 1858, ". . . this republic can exist forever divided into free and slave States. . . ." Twelve thousand people attended this segment of the seven-part touring debate between the "Little Giant" and the challenger for his Senate seat, Abraham Lincoln; the tour's aggregate audience would be about seventy-eight thousand, and the newspapers would carry the debaters' statements to the entire nation.

At Quincy, Lincoln rose and thanked Douglas for revealing that his "policy in regard to . . . slavery contemplates that it shall last forever." His somber irony pointed up Douglas' chief liability, an essentially cynical, amoral attitude toward slavery, which he thought of only as an issue that interfered with the nation's expansion. Apparently blind to the backlash that stung neutrals in the 1850's, Douglas had long held that territorial slavery should be left up to the settlers. This "popular-sovereignty" proposal was the basis of his Kansas-Nebraska bill of 1854; since Douglas wanted the Nebraska territory organized (thus clearing the way for a transcontinental railroad that would benefit Northern speculators, of which he was one), he wooed Southern support for the bill by including in it repeal of the Missouri Compromise. The bill became law, but anti-Douglas demonstrations in the North and the subsequent violence in Kansas indicated that the father of popular sovereignty had sired an unmanageable son. When, in 1857, Buchanan supported Kansas' fraudulent Lecompton constitution, Douglas (who knew that most of his constituents opposed the proslavery document) led the fight for con-gressional rejection of the constitution. "I have taken a through ticket," he said, snapping defiance at Buchanan and the Southern Democrats, "and checked my baggage."

Although Douglas was keenly ambitious, it would be unfair to say that his popular-sovereignty concept had been devised solely for political or economic gain. After his election to Congress from Illinois in 1843, he blossomed into a popular, persuasive nationalist of the Henry Clay mold. Short, muscular, modishly dressed, and flamboyant, he was to his contemporaries a "steam engine in britches," as he urged that all of Oregon be taken, supported the Mexican War, and guided the Compromise of 1850 through Congress. But Douglas miscalculated the mood of the nation, and his stand on slavery made him an agent of party schism. When, during a debate with Lincoln at Freeport, he suggested that the Dred Scott decision could be circumvented by the states and territories, he calcified the rift between Northern and Southern Democrats. In the senatorial election of 1858, Douglas lost the popular vote, but was re-elected because the Democrats retained narrow control of the legislature; his seat was saved but his party was shattered.

Two years later Douglas was the presidential candidate of the Northern and Western Democrats. He knew that he could not win, but he toured the South, pleading for loyalty to the next President, ignoring the jeers and eggs that were directed at him. In 1861 Douglas bid every American to "rally around the flag"; that June, typhoid fever claimed the life of the forty-eight-year-old gamecock who had helped dress the national stage for secession and who, in his debates with Lincoln, had helped make a President.

Senator Stephen A. Douglas, the "Great Debater"

The 1860 campaign flag above deploys its thirty-three stars—one for each
state then in the Union—to form one large star with stars at each angle.

The poster above, issued in September of 1860 and obviously pro-Lincoln,
shows him easily outsprinting (from left) Bell, Breckinridge, and Douglas.

LINCOLN:
PRESIDENT-ELECT

Only events can make a President," said a cryptic Abraham Lincoln in 1858—and by May of 1860 he was the Republican candidate, an almost sure winner against the fragmented Democrats. In the interim he had toured widely, his speeches had been published, and he had kept in touch with party leaders; and while Southern saber rattling was met by radical denunciations from many Republican hopefuls, Lincoln had remained moderate, opposing only slavery's territorial extension and deploring John Brown's raid. Even so, his nomination was not assured. His managers had to pack the convention hall with leather-lunged boosters and wheel and deal with delegations from the key states. The subsequent campaign was not lacking the usual hoop-la and smear, but it was dominated by the slavery issue; Lincoln became the most sectionally chosen President ever. The Atlanta *Confederacy* trumpeted, "Whether . . . Pennsylvania Avenue is paved ten fathoms deep with mangled bodies . . . the South will never submit to . . . the inauguration of Abraham Lincoln." But even as the Cotton South seceded, Lincoln remained as firm as "a chain of steel" on slavery's extension. With Southern delegates having walked out of the Peace Conference in February, the new President took office on a day which was, portentously, now sunny, now cloudy, and cold and windy throughout.

HANNIBAL HAMLIN

Hannibal Hamlin, a prominent Maine Republican and a leading opponent of slavery, was the logical choice for Lincoln's running mate in the election of 1860. Formerly associated with the Jacksonian Democrats, Hamlin renounced his allegiance in 1856 over the issue of slavery and joined the new Republican party. His political career began when as a young lawyer in Hampden, Maine, he was named to the state legislature, where he served for five years. In 1842 he was elected to Congress, and in 1848 he became a United States senator. After quitting the Democratic party, he was elected governor of Maine on the Republican ticket in 1856. He served in his new post for only a few weeks before resigning to renew his antislavery crusade in the Senate. Elected to the Vice Presidency in 1861, he soon became impatient with Lincoln's cautious approach to the problems of emancipation. In 1863 he complained: "The slow and unsatisfactory movements of the government do not meet my approbation. . . ." As convention time approached, Hamlin's association with the radical elements of Congress worked against him, and he lost the bid for renomination. In 1868 he was again elected to the Senate, where he served until his appointment as minister to Spain in 1881. Returning to his native state, he was influential in the Republican party organization until his death at the age of eighty-two in 1891.

THE NEW YORK

WHOLE NO. 8982. SECOND EDITION—SATURDAY, APRIL 13,

THE WAR BEGUN.

Very Exciting News from Charleston.

Important Correspondence Between General Beauregard, Major Anderson and the Southern Secretary of War.

The Summons to Major Anderson to Surrender.

MAJOR ANDERSON'S REFUSAL.

Bombardment of Fort Sumter Commenced.

Terrible Fire from the Secessionists' Batteries.

Brilliant Defence of Maj. Anderson and His Gallant Garrison.

Reckless Bravery of the Confederate States Troops.

SIXTEEN HOURS FIGHTING.

Breaches in the Walls of Fort Sumter.

Several of Major Anderson's Guns Silenced.

Partial Cessation of the Firing for the Night.

THE SCENE OF

Charleston and Its Defences---Plan of the Harb and Moultrie, Cummings Point Iro Floating Battery and O

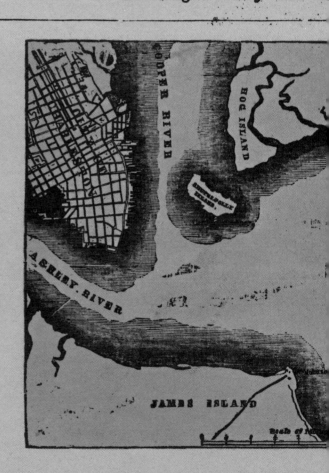

livesand at every shot jump upon the rampartobserve the effect, and then jump down, cheeng.

A rty on the Stevens battery are said to have played game of the hottest fire.

The xcitement in the community is indescribable. With the very first boom of the gun thousands rused from their beds to the harbor front, and all day every available place has been tranged by ladies and gentlemen, viewing the spectacle through their

Major Anderson is busy repairing damages. He received twenty-nine full shots from Stevens' battery alone, making the bricks fly from the walls in all directions.

It is estimated that from twelve to eighteen hundred balls and shells were fired during the day. Over one hundred shells took effect inside the fort.

Orders have been issued to send Major Anderson a bomb from all the batteries every twenty

It is the ba

The renew tempt arrang

The are re Tro

ᴇRALD

—PAST ONE O'CLOCK P. M.

RATIONS.

ᴴg the Position of Forts Sumter
, Fort Johnson, the
ᴵfications.

war vessels are outside

April 12—Evening.
the night, but will be
morning, unless an at-
the fort, which ample
de to repel.

, and a third steamer,

ery train.

CHARLESTON AND ITS DEFENCES.

The news of the bombardment of Fort Sumter by the
Confederate forces, which we publish this morning, in-
duces us to give a full description of the scene of operations, embracing the city of Charleston, its harbor and
fortifications. The plans of the forts and batteries, showing the stronghold of Major Anderson and the position of
the attacking forces under General Beauregard, cannot
fail to interest our readers.

FORT SUMTER—THE STRONGHOLD OF MAJOR AN-
DERSON.

THE WAR BEGINS

President Lincoln had vowed to "hold, occupy, and possess" federal property, and Fort Sumter in Charleston Harbor became a symbol of the North's determination. If Major Robert Anderson and his small force were to surrender Sumter, the North would in effect be recognizing the Confederacy and the disunion it had been denying. But Anderson was short of food, and Lincoln had to decide whether to precipitate a crisis by provisioning the fort. He refused to be stampeded into a hasty decision—not by a Cabinet that advised against sending supplies nor by a Secretary of State who proposed a foreign war to reunite the nation. Lincoln hoped to arrange an eventual withdrawal from Sumter that would keep Virginia in the Union ("A State for a fort is no bad business"), but he received no promises from Richmond. And because Secretary Seward, acting on his own, had advised the Confederacy of Sumter's imminent evacuation, the South regarded Lincoln's ultimate decision to provision the fort as a broken promise. On April 11, Anderson refused a demand that he surrender, saying that he would do so only when—and if—food ran out. He was then told that shore batteries would open fire. Early the next morning they did, and the Civil War began. The fort surrendered on the 13th, as festive Charlestonians watched the bombardment. None seemed to recall Andrew Jackson's dire warning issued during the Nullification Crisis of 1832: "Disunion by armed force is treason. Are you really ready to incur its guilt?"

The map of Charleston Harbor, left, showed the North what Anderson was up against. Sumter was encircled by Rebel batteries from Fort Moultrie and Castle Pinckney—in Confederate hands since late December—and from Fort Johnson and Cummings Point (off the map to the right). Only one defender died in the thirty-four-hour bombardment of Sumter; he was killed when a federal cannon exploded.

430　On July 21, 1861, at Bull Run in northern Virginia, North and South clashed in the first major battle of the war. The 1889 lithograph above mistakenly shows the Union's "Fire Zouaves" in their gaudy dress uniforms, and more erroneously, gives the impres-

sion that there was some semblance of order on the battlefield. Actually, Bull Run was a confused and bloody encounter between two green armies, and a victory for the Confederacy, to the horror of those Washingtonians who had come out to watch a federal triumph.

HEROES OF THE UNION

GEORGE THOMAS

Asked once if some dead soldiers should be buried according to their state of origin, General George Thomas said, "No, no. Mix them up. I am tired of State rights." But doubts of the Virginia-born officer's loyalty persisted, enhanced by Thomas' chronic sluggishness. (He often catnapped through councils of war.) Not until late in the Civil War would all question of his allegiance, ability, and courage be swept away. Thomas, who had served continuously in the Army since his graduation from West Point in 1840, earned the sobriquet "the Rock of Chickamauga" for his determined stand there in September, 1863, amidst a defeat which sent the rest of the Army of the Cumberland scrambling toward Chattanooga. Promoted to brigadier general, he took over the command of the unstable William Rosecrans. Thomas worked smoothly with Grant and Sherman in breaking the Confederate siege of Chattanooga; his own troops secured the victory with a daring assault on Missionary Ridge on November 25, 1863. Having led Sherman's vanguard into Atlanta, Thomas was assigned to prevent John Hood's Confederate troops from slipping north to aid Lee. Battle was decisively joined in Nashville on December 15 and 16, 1864, after what Lincoln had considered too long a delay. But General Hood was defeated by Thomas in one of the war's major routs.

WILLIAM T. SHERMAN

General William Tecumseh Sherman believed in total war. In 1863 he wrote that "talk of compromise is bosh" and urged the North to hound the South to its "innermost recesses" to make its people "so sick of war that generations would pass away before they would again appeal to it." A brooding and temperamental man, Sherman had firm friendships with Southerners and espoused a liberal peace. But he felt that waging war in the Confederate hinterland would enervate local morale and hasten the end of bloodshed. After graduating from West Point in 1840, Sherman had tried several civilian pursuits in the 1850's, none successfully. He re-entered the Army in 1861 and was widely criticized for his role in the early campaigns, but he was vindicated at Vicksburg and Chattanooga and was commander of the Western armies by 1864. That year's plan was simple: Grant was to contain Lee in the North while Sherman crushed the Southern opposition. By September 1, he had beaten a bloody path to Atlanta; soon sixty thousand men would begin their march to the sea under the man Carl Sandburg called a "lean, restless, hawk-eyed rider of war and apostle of destruction." Georgia despoiled, Sherman swung north; the vise tightened, and the Confederacy was doomed. Sherman retired as general of the Army in 1883 and died in 1891, at the age of seventy-one.

PHILIP SHERIDAN

"Little Phil" Sheridan, commander of the cavalry of the Army of the Potomac, was up for promotion early in 1864. Although he had distinguished himself the year before, notably at Chickamauga and Chattanooga, most of official Washington knew only that the short, slight Ohioan looked more like a jockey than a general. But U. S. Grant had noted Sheridan's leadership in combat and his abilities as an intuitive strategist: in August he was given command of the newly formed Army of the Shenandoah. That autumn Sheridan thrice defeated the forces of Jubal Early—once, at Cedar Run, by audaciously rallying his men to turn a near rout into a signal victory. So ordered by Grant, he despoiled the Shenandoah Valley, with staggering losses to the Confederacy of food and munitions. He had given Lincoln's bid for re-election a much-needed boost; the President later told him he had always felt "a cavalryman should be at least six feet four high, but I have changed my mind— five feet four will do in a pinch." Sheridan, by then a major general in the regular army, helped apply the *coup de grâce* to Lee's forces the following spring. After the war he commanded the military forces in Louisiana and Texas, later serving as military governor and leading operations against hostile Indians. Sheridan was elevated to the rank of full general before he died in 1888.

DAVID FARRAGUT

Captain David Farragut, sixty years old in the winter of 1862, was not hopeful of realizing his ambition to become a distinguished naval leader. He had been a midshipman in the War of 1812 and had served routine tours since; not even the Mexican War had brought the active duty he so keenly sought. A firm Unionist, Farragut had moved north from Virginia in 1861; a year later he had his chance: he was given command of the West Gulf Blockading Squadron, assigned to capture New Orleans and open the Mississippi. After ineffectually bombarding two forts defending the city, Farragut decided on April 24, 1862, to sail past the forts, contrary to his orders. Successful, he defeated the flotilla lying between him and New Orleans; he took the city, and the forts surrendered. Farragut was then elevated to the newly created rank of rear admiral. In August of 1864 he engineered the capture of Mobile Bay, the last gap in the blockade. Again he faced fortresses, a flotilla, and mines, but again his sagacious daring produced victory. Sailing under the guns of Fort Morgan, he thundered, "Damn the torpedoes [mines]!" The fleet followed him through, and the victory at Mobile paralleled that of New Orleans. Farragut, a national hero, was commissioned admiral in 1866; the next year he led a naval squadron on a good-will tour of European ports.

In the drawing on the right, the President and General Winfield Scott review a regiment of three-year volunteers marching down Pennsylvania Avenue early in the war. The Commander in Chief was always eager to see troops as they came through the Capital. According to Robert Lincoln, the presidential carriage once stopped to allow a line of soldiers to pass. Lincoln called out to a group of nearby workmen, "What is that, boys?"—in hopes they knew the soldiers' home state. The reply: "It's a regiment, you damned old fool," and the President had a hearty laugh at his own expense.

Below, the New York Excelsior Brigade makes its charge in the inconclusive Battle of Fair Oaks during the abortive Peninsular Campaign of early 1862.

"PEGGING AWAY"

I don't amount to pig tracks in the War Department," said President Lincoln, but he was there, day after weary day, poring over wires from the front, answering them with encouragement or gentle admonition, always feeling the anguish of fraternal war, firmly resolved "to keep pegging away." Some of his wartime measures were severely criticized, notably the suspension of habeas corpus and the national conscription act, but he saw them as essential to victory, to "proving that popular government is not an absurdity." He ached for peace, but had it for less than two of the nearly fifty months he served; he wielded the sword longer than any other American Commander in Chief. Finally he found an able leader and left the war to him. When visitors complained that General Grant would not tell them about the Army's movements, President Lincoln said, "Neither will he tell me."

The skirmish at Antietam, above, is by Alfred R. Waud, as are the other sketches on these pages. The English illustrator, a "war artist" for Harper's, *was a familiar figure in Union camps throughout the conflict.*

THE OTHER PRESIDENT

No man is fit to take hold," wrote Henry Adams about both the North and the South, "who is not as cool as death." But whereas Lincoln rose to greatness as leader of the Union, circumstances and his own character conspired against Jefferson Davis, the President of the Confederacy. He was not the South's first choice for leadership: Alexander Stephens, a Georgia congressman, was offered the Presidency initially, but refused because he would not "strike the first blow." Davis himself accepted the office reluctantly ("as a man might speak of a sentence of death," said his wife); he would have preferred a military commission. Although he had been successful in politics, serving in Congress in the 1840's and 1850's and as Secretary of War under Franklin Pierce, he was proudest of his Army record. Born in Kentucky and raised in Mississippi, Davis had won appointment to West Point in 1824. Although he had served without distinction in the Black Hawk War in the early 1830's, he had been acclaimed a hero during the Mexican War when he made a stand at Buena Vista that saved Zachary Taylor from defeat. Davis' first wife was Taylor's daughter, who had died a few months after their marriage, in 1835. Ten years later, Davis married into the Mississippi aristocracy, embracing all its social and philosophical tenets. As a plantation owner and as a politician, he came to regard the South as a country within a country and served as the region's spokesman in Washington. He was a tall, slim, elegant man noted for "the grace of his diction, and the rare charm of his voice"; as Carl Schurz said, he had "that kind of dignity which does not invite familiar approach...."

Accompanying that dignity, unfortunately, was an imperious and humorless egotism.

At first, Davis opposed total secession, espousing a "dominion status" for the South. But when Mississippi seceded, he resigned his Senate seat and on February 18, 1861, was inaugurated as provisional President of the Confederacy; later that year he was elected to a full six-year term. He headed a would-be nation whose economy was ill-suited to war; the Northern blockade prevented European aid; and the Confederacy's fiscal structure was chaotic. But Davis himself was no help. Because of his thwarted military ambitions, he repeatedly thrust his own stratagems upon his generals, often hampering field operations. And his uncompromising federalist viewpoint gave rise to political antipathies. As he strove for centralization, favoring general conscription and the suspension of the writ of habeas corpus, many in the government came to regard him as a despot, unsympathetic to states' rights. The Richmond *Whig* spoke for the opposition: "This Confederacy is not a nation, but a league of nations." But to the end Davis maintained "we are fighting for independence, and that, or extermination, we *will* have." He refused to negotiate for peace on any basis other than between "the two countries," bearing out Lincoln's remark that "he affords us no excuse to deceive ourselves." After the war, Davis supported himself as a private businessman and author until his death at eighty-two in 1889. Although he had been indicted for treason and had served two years in prison, he was never brought to trial. To those who insisted that Davis be hanged, Lincoln had replied softly, "Judge not, that ye not be judged."

Jefferson Davis, by Swiss artist Carl Gutherz

The advertisement on the right was not unlike the ones young Abe Lincoln saw on flatboat trips to New Orleans in 1828 and 1831. Legend has it that his reaction to a slave auction there was, "If I ever get a chance to hit that thing, I'll hit it hard." His Emancipation Proclamation did not hit it all that hard, but it paved the way for the Thirteenth Amendment, ratified eight months after his murder. The allegorical painting below, by A. A. Lamb, was made in 1865. Lincoln, escorted by some Union soldiers and heralded by Liberty, tenders his proclamation to a crowd of unfettered Negroes while the sun breaks through storm clouds over the Capitol.

EMANCIPATION

Issued in September, 1862, the Preliminary Emancipation Proclamation was clearly a warning—and an offer. Confederate states renouncing rebellion by electing federal congressmen could retain slavery; elsewhere in the South it would be outlawed. Only two Louisiana districts complied. Fearing further secession, Lincoln chose to leave border-state slavery alone, thereby infuriating the abolitionists. Republican losses in the elections that fall indicated dissent to the new policy. Even Lincoln knew that the decree was as enforceable in the South as "the Pope's bull against the comet!" But he stood firm. The proclamation, enacted in January, prevented European recognition of the South. And although many Northerners were at first unenthusiastic ("I don't think enough of the Niggar to go and fight for them," said one Ohio soldier), Negroes were soon in uniform, fighting for themselves. And gradually more Northerners began to regard the tragic war as a crusade for freedom as well as for preservation of the Union.

Characteristic of the South's propaganda during the Civil War is the vicious drawing above, entitled "Under the Veil," which portrays Lincoln as a Negro. The Richmond Enquirer asked rhetorically, "What shall we call him? Coward, assassin, savage, murderer of women . . . ?" It settled for "Fiend."

The 1864 campaign item above was a child's "ball-shot" game featuring Lincoln and prominent Union generals. The cover of the contemporary songbook on the right is embellished by scenes from the President's early life.

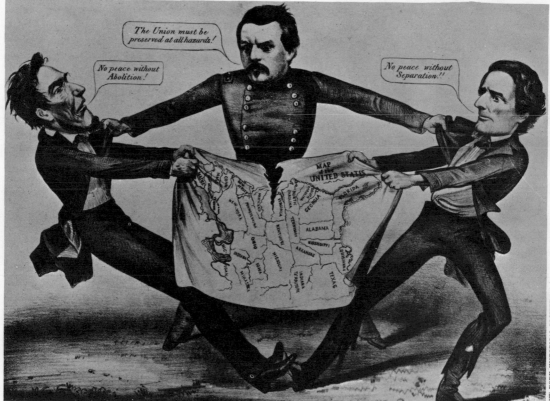

George McClellan (center, above) is depicted as the answer to the schism created by Lincoln and Davis. In the event of McClellan's election, Lincoln planned to work with him to try to end the war quickly. Secretary Seward later remarked that McClellan would have said, " 'Yes, yes' . . . and would have done nothing at all."

TEARS AND LAUGHTER

Under Lincoln the White House was full of activity. Initial swarms of office seekers gave way to queues of congressmen, soldiers, and petitioners to whom the accessible President listened patiently in his daily "public opinion baths." There were regular receptions and levees, which Lincoln endured (calling ceremonial gloves "cruelty to animals"), but which his wife craved. Troubled Mary Lincoln was a mixed blessing as First Lady. Rumors that she was a spy (she had kin in both armies) distressed her already unstable mind. She had severe headaches, periods of deep depression, outbursts of temper; her prolonged agonizing over young Willie's death from typhoid fever prompted Lincoln to threaten to place her in an asylum. The grieving mother consulted spiritual mediums, and more than once an incredulous Abraham Lincoln witnessed séances in the Red Room. Passionately bent on being Washington's social leader, Mary spent money lavishly—in four months she bought three hundred pairs of gloves. She exceeded a White House refurbishing budget by seven thousand dollars, and her clothing debts ran to twenty-seven thousand. She had good cause to rejoice when her husband defeated George McClellan in the election of 1864. Often the theater or opera took Lincoln's mind off his troubles, and he usually carried a copy of a Shakespearean play to bed with him. A constant tonic was Tad, his youngest son—active, excitable, ubiquitous. He sometimes sat on his father's knee during policy discussions; he often slept in his father's bed. When Tad sentenced a doll to death for insubordination, his father solemnly wrote: "The doll Jack is pardoned. By order of the President. A. Lincoln." Tad once startled some visitors by driving a pair of pet goats through the East Room. Like any other wartime home, the White House was a place of bitter tears and grateful laughter.

MESERVE COLLECTION

The picture above shows Mary Lincoln around 1863. In later years, with a husband murdered and three sons dead, her mind gave way. She thought herself impoverished, yet continued to spend wildly. She would murmur, "I am afraid; I am afraid," with no apparent reason. When Robert Lincoln felt it necessary to have her committed, she accused him of robbery and "wicked conduct." Adjudged insane in 1875, she was, however, later found to be competent.

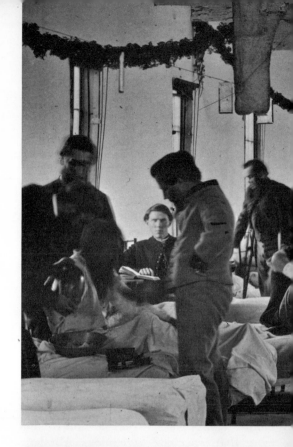

THE END IN SIGHT

The President's face, reported Horace Greeley in March of 1865, "was haggard with care and seamed with thought and trouble." Well it might have been, for the past few months had been as strenuous as any he had endured. He had told Congress in December that he would stop prosecuting the war "whenever it shall have ceased on the part of those who began it." But he realized the South "would accept nothing short of severance of the Union," so—"casual as a locomotive," in Carl Sandburg's phrase—he called for three hundred thousand more men to fight the staggered Confederacy. He was equally intent on implementing emancipation. The House vote on the Thirteenth Amendment would be extremely close, and he issued an imperative to two congressmen: "I am President of the United States . . . and I expect you to procure those votes." They did as they were told. In the spirit of his recent Inaugural Address, Lincoln planned for the liberal treatment of an enemy whose surrender was imminent. To his commander at evacuated Richmond he said, "I'd let 'em up easy, let 'em up easy." Four years of war had exhausted Lincoln, but he could not find the balm for "the *tired* spot." He had told Harriet Beecher Stowe: "I shall never live to see peace. This war is killing me." Early in April, Lincoln was "strangely annoyed" by a dream in which he saw a catafalque in the East Room. "Who is dead . . . ?" asked the President. A military guard replied that it was Lincoln himself, "killed by an assassin!"

To the right, above, is a photograph of wounded soldiers in Washington's Carver Hospital; at least 375,000 men were wounded, but not killed, in the war. At right is a view of Charleston after Sherman's men had burned it early in 1865. "The men 'had it in' for [South Carolina]," wrote one Northern officer, "and they took it out in their own way."

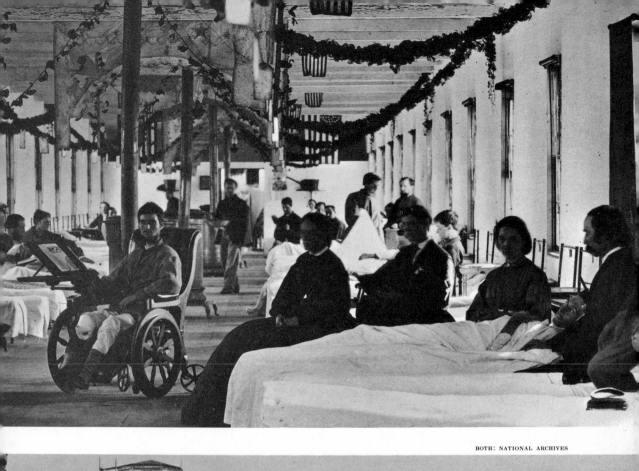

ASSASSINATION

"Our country owe[s] all her troubles to him," wrote John Wilkes Booth shortly before he murdered Abraham Lincoln, "and God simply made me the instrument of His punishment." But Booth was less an avenging angel than a guilt-ridden Southerner who had done nothing for the cause. Now, with an egotistical thirst for immortality whittling away at his sanity, he burned to redeem himself. (Co-conspirators were Lewis Paine, George Atzerodt, and David Herold—a motley, drifting crew who intended to kill William Seward and Andrew Johnson while Booth performed in the scheme's mad limelight—and Mary Surratt, who had sheltered them. These four would be hanged in July.) On Good Friday of 1865 Booth learned Lincoln would be at Ford's Theater that evening. Quickly he arranged for a horse, bored a peephole in the door of the President's box—and took time to tell a hotel clerk that there would be "some fine acting" at Ford's that night. When the time came, Booth coolly flashed his card at presidential guard John Parker, who accepted him as a halfhearted watchdog would accept a burglar with a scrap of meat. Seconds later, a handmade lead ball just under a half inch in diameter augered through Lincoln's brain. Booth broke his left shin in his leap from the box to the stage, but he was still able to escape. A doctor, Charles Leale, rushed up from the audience and removed a blood clot from the President's wound, slightly easing the pressure on the brain. Leale's prognosis: "It is impossible for him to recover." For nearly nine hours in a nearby rooming house, Lincoln lay unconscious, his life seeping away. The doctors were as helpless as the stunned dignitaries who crowded into the nine by fifteen room. Secretary of State Seward, stabbed at his home, would live; but in the morning, as a steady, cold rain fell, Abraham Lincoln died.

Harper's Weekly

The drawing above mistakenly shows Booth assailing Lincoln from the side. He actually came up from the rear, took careful aim at the back of the head (three inches from and in line with Lincoln's left ear), and fired his brass derringer. Opposite is one of the last pictures of Lincoln.

THE ROAD HOME

The search for Booth was on, spurred by a War Department offer of $50,000 for his capture; the Radical press was accused of having incited the assassination; die-hard "Copperheads" gloated. But the citizenry at large was stunned. The nation's front doorways wore crepe, and men wept quietly with their wives and uncomprehending children. It was a silent, pervasive grief, ultimate and inconsolable. Easter sermons that April 16, 1865, were calls for retribution, panegyrics for a leader lost, apologies from preachers who could not find words. Thousands viewed the body in the White House—dignitaries, wounded soldiers, citizens black and white—as did tens of thousands more later in the week under the Capitol's new dome. On Friday, April 21, the casket was aboard a nine-car train that retraced to Springfield the route President-elect Lincoln had traveled fifty months before. The mourners varied—subdued by rain at Baltimore, nearly panicking in a mad crush in Philadelphia—but their numbers were impressive (at Newark, New Jersey, they stood a mile square). The train was in Albany on the twenty-sixth, the day that John Wilkes Booth, cornered by soldiers in a burning barn in Virginia, was mortally shot. His enigmatic last words: "Useless. Useless." On the train went, through Ohio, Indiana, to Chicago and, at last, home. On the fourth of May, Abraham Lincoln was buried, Henry Ward Beecher's peroration of Easter Sunday yet echoing, "Give him place, oh, ye prairies. . . . Ye winds . . . of the West, chant his requiem!"

The lantern slide on the left shows the funeral procession inching its way down Broadway toward New York's City Hall on April 24, 1865. The next day, with scalpers selling window space to spectators, nearly one hundred thousand marched to the depot to see the body of the President on its way.

FACTS IN SUMMARY: ABRAHAM LINCOLN

CHRONOLOGY

UNITED STATES		LINCOLN			
Madison inaugurated as President	1809	*Born February 12*	Clay's compromise	1850	*Son Edward dies*
War with Great Britain	1812		*Uncle Tom's Cabin* published	1852	
Monroe elected President	1816	*Moves with family to Indiana*	Pierce elected President		
Jackson elected President	1828		Kansas-Nebraska Act	1854	*Denounces slavery in "Peoria Speech"*
Webster-Hayne debates	1830	*Moves to Illinois*	Republican party formed		
	1831	*Works in Offut's store*		1855	*Runs unsuccessfully for U.S. Senate*
Jackson re-elected	1832	*Serves as volunteer in Black Hawk War*	Civil war in Kansas	1856	
		Runs unsuccessfully for Illinois assembly	Buchanan elected President		
Jackson removes deposits from Bank of the U.S.	1833	*Appointed postmaster for New Salem*	Dred Scott decision	1857	
		Appointed deputy county surveyor		1858	*Debates with Douglas during campaign for Senate seat*
	1834	*Elected to Illinois general assembly*	Brown's raid at Harpers Ferry	1859	
Van Buren elected President	1836	*Re-elected to Illinois general assembly*	South Carolina secedes from Union	1860	*Elected President*
		Admitted to the bar	Fort Sumter fired upon	1861	*Orders Fort Sumter reprovisioned*
Financial panic	1837	*Moves to Springfield*	First Bull Run		*Issues call for 75,000 volunteers*
Webster-Ashburton Treaty	1842	*Marries Mary Todd*	*Trent* affair		*Orders blockade of South*
Polk elected President	1844		Battle of Shiloh	1862	*Issues Preliminary Emancipation Proclamation*
War with Mexico	1846	*Elected to House of Representatives*	Second Confiscation Act passed		
Oregon boundary settled		*Opposes Mexican War*	Battle of Antietam		*Son William dies*
Taylor elected President	1848	*Campaigns for Taylor*	Battle of Fredericksburg		

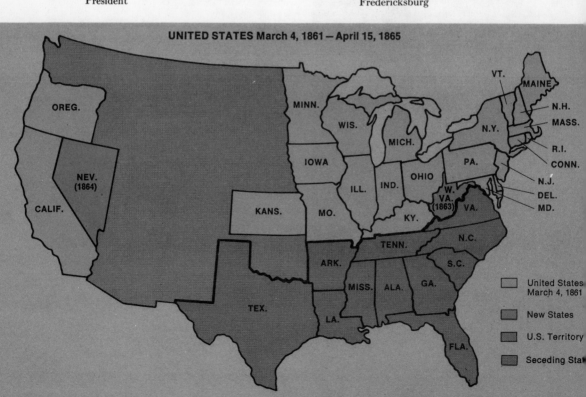

UNITED STATES March 4, 1861 — April 15, 1865

OREG.
MINN.
VT.
MAINE
N.H.
WIS.
MICH.
N.Y.
MASS.
IOWA
OHIO
PA.
R.I.
CONN.
NEV. (1864)
ILL. IND.
W. VA. (1863)
N.J.
DEL.
MD.
CALIF.
KANS. MO.
KY.
VA.
TENN.
N.C.
ARK.
S.C.
MISS. ALA. GA.
TEX.
LA.
FLA.

United States March 4, 1861

New States

U.S. Territory

Seceding States

VERMONT HISTORICAL SOCIETY
Montpelier, Vermont 05602

VHS News and Notes
January, 1970
Volume 21 No 4

Non Profit-Org
U. S. POSTAGE
1.6c PAID
Montpelier, Vt.
PERMIT NO. 83

We don't know her name, and we don't know when or where this photograph was snapped, but it lies in the pictorial files of the Vermont Historical Society as evidence that Vermonters have long known how to enjoy themselves in winter.

For another view of gracefulness on skiis, take a look at the rear cover of this issue of News And Notes.

Self-important city folks who cavort on weekends at Vermont ski lodges may think they discovered the pleasures of skiing before the natives did, but these pictures should deflate any arguments of that kind.

Conscription Act	1863	*Issues Emancipation Proclamation*
Chancellorsville		
Vicksburg Campaign		*Delivers Gettysburg Address*
Battle of Gettysburg		
Battle of Chattanooga		*Proposes moderate Reconstruction policy*
Battle of the Wilderness	1864	*Names Grant general in chief of Union armies*
Spotsylvania		*Re-elected President*
Fall of Petersburg	1865	*Visits Richmond*
Lee surrenders at Appomattox		*Shot by John Wilkes Booth*
		Dies April 15

BIOGRAPHICAL FACTS

BIRTH: Hardin County, Ky., Feb. 12, 1809

ANCESTRY: English

FATHER: Thomas Lincoln; b. Rockingham County, Va., 1778; d. Coles County, Ill., Jan. 15, 1851

FATHER'S OCCUPATIONS: Farmer; carpenter

MOTHER: Nancy Hanks Lincoln; b. Va., Feb. 5, 1784; Spencer County, Ind., Oct. 5, 1818

STEPMOTHER: Sarah Bush Johnston; b. Hardin County, Ky., Dec. 12, 1788; d. Charleston, Ill., April 10, 1869

BROTHER: Thomas (b. and d. 1812)

SISTER: Sarah (1807–1828)

WIFE: Mary Todd; b. Lexington, Ky., Dec. 13, 1818; d. Springfield, Ill., July 16, 1882

MARRIAGE: Springfield, Ill., Nov. 4, 1842

CHILDREN: Robert Todd (1843–1926); Edward Baker (1846–1850); William Wallace (1850–1862); Thomas ("Tad") (1853–1871)

HOME: Eighth and Jackson streets, Springfield, Ill.

EDUCATION: Local tutors; self-educated

OCCUPATIONS BEFORE PRESIDENCY: Store clerk; store owner; ferry pilot; surveyor; postmaster; lawyer

MILITARY SERVICE: Served in volunteer company three months during Black Hawk War (1832)

PRE-PRESIDENTIAL OFFICES: Member Illinois General Assembly; Member U.S. House of Representatives

AGE AT INAUGURATION: 52

DEATH: Washington, D.C., April 15, 1865

PLACE OF BURIAL: Oak Ridge Cemetery, Springfield

ELECTION OF 1860

CANDIDATES	ELECTORAL VOTE	POPULAR VOTE
Abraham Lincoln Republican	180	1,865,593
Stephen Douglas Democratic	12	1,382,713
John C. Breckinridge Southern Democratic	72	848,356
John Bell Constitutional Union	39	592,906

FIRST ADMINISTRATION

INAUGURATION: March 4, 1861; the Capitol, Washington, D.C.

VICE PRESIDENT: Hannibal Hamlin

SECRETARY OF STATE: William H. Seward

SECRETARY OF THE TREASURY: Salmon P. Chase; William P. Fessenden (from July 5, 1864)

SECRETARY OF WAR: Simon Cameron; Edwin M. Stanton (from Jan. 20, 1862)

ATTORNEY GENERAL: Edward Bates; James Speed (from Dec. 5, 1864)

POSTMASTER GENERAL: Montgomery Blair; William Dennison (from Oct. 1, 1864)

SECRETARY OF THE NAVY: Gideon Welles

SECRETARY OF THE INTERIOR: Caleb B. Smith; John P. Usher (from Jan. 1, 1863)

SUPREME COURT APPOINTMENTS: Noah H. Swayne (1862); Samuel F. Miller (1862); David Davis (1862); Stephen J. Field (1863); Salmon P. Chase, Chief Justice (1864)

37th CONGRESS (March 4, 1861–March 4, 1863):
Senate: 31 Republicans; 10 Democrats; 8 Others
House: 105 Republicans; 43 Democrats; 30 Others

38th CONGRESS (March 4, 1863–March 4, 1865):
Senate: 36 Republicans; 9 Democrats; 5 Others
House: 102 Republicans; 75 Democrats; 9 Others

STATES ADMITTED: West Virginia (1863); Nevada (1864)

END OF PRESIDENTIAL TERM: March 4, 1865

ELECTION OF 1864

(Because eleven Southern states had seceded from the Union and did not participate in the presidential election, eighty-one electoral votes were not cast.)

CANDIDATES	ELECTORAL VOTE	POPULAR VOTE
Abraham Lincoln National Union	212	2,206,938
George McClellan Democratic	21	1,803,787

SECOND ADMINISTRATION

INAUGURATION: March 4, 1865; the Capitol, Washington, D.C.

VICE PRESIDENT: Andrew Johnson

SECRETARY OF STATE: William H. Seward

SECRETARY OF THE TREASURY: Hugh McCulloch

SECRETARY OF WAR: Edwin M. Stanton

ATTORNEY GENERAL: James Speed

POSTMASTER GENERAL: William Dennison

SECRETARY OF THE NAVY: Gideon Welles

SECRETARY OF THE INTERIOR: John P. Usher

39th CONGRESS (March 4, 1865–March 4, 1867):
Senate: 42 Unionists; 10 Democrats
House: 149 Unionists; 42 Democrats

END OF PRESIDENTIAL TERM: April 15, 1865